BREATHWORK

Swami Ambikananda is a yoga teacher, acupuncturist and herbalist with a private practice in Reading, UK. Many years ago she came to the realization that without dealing with the breath and the breathing habits of each patient, healing possibilities were reduced. She runs 'conscious breathing' workshops throughout the UK four times a year.

THORSONS
PRINCIPLES
OF

BREATHWORK

SWAMI AMBIKANANDA SARASWATI

Thorsons
An Imprint of HarperCollins*Publishers*

Thorsons
An Imprint of HarperCollins*Publishers*
77–85 Fulham Palace Road,
Hammersmith, London W6 8JB

Published by Thorsons 1999
1 3 5 7 9 10 8 6 4 2

A catalogue record for this book
is available from the British Library

ISBN 0 7225 3830 8

Text illustrations by Peter Cox Associates

Printed and bound in Great Britain by
Caledonian International Book Manufacturing Ltd, Glasgow

DEDICATED TO
SWAMI VENKATESANANDA SARASWATI

CONTENTS

ACKNOWLEDGEMENTS

M y deepest thanks go to Wilmette Brown for her editing, but most of all for always helping me to say what I wanted to when I could not find the words. To Charlotte Howard of Fox and Howard Literary Agency for keeping the faith. To Dr Philip James, senior lecturer in Occupational Medicine at the Wolfson Hyperbaric Medicine Unit, University of Dundee for his kind and helpful guidance during the writing of the chapter on Hyperbaric Oxygen.

A BREATHING BEING

Nothing in biology makes sense except in the light of evolution.

THEODOSIUS DOBZHANSKY

N one of us needs a manual or a teacher to tell us how to take our first breath and how to carry on breathing. After emerging from the womb each of us signals our independence with a breath and a sound. That is the moment our individual life begins. At the moment of birth, muscle, nerve and organ tissue instinctively respond to the body's changed environment to orchestrate that first inhalation. From then on we live with this intimate exchange with the earth's atmosphere, breathing in and breathing out approximately 18 times a minute, 1,080 times an hour, 25,920 times each 24 hour cycle – for the rest of our lives.

In common with all other life on this planet, we humans take energy from our environment and by the power of our own alchemy transform it from one thing into another. One of the gases we inhale is oxygen. It is the gas that gave rise to the extraordinary process of evolution through which we appeared on earth and it remains *our primary source of energy*. We can survive for some days without water, for weeks without food, but only for a few moments without oxygen before major systems start to break down irrevocably. Each and every one of the 75 trillion cells in our body absorbs the oxygen we breathe in from the surrounding atmosphere and, through the process of metabolism, produces carbon dioxide which we breathe out.

An enormous amount of research has been done this century by people dedicated to finding out how we can make better use of our bodies. Great bodywork systems, like the Alexander Technique of F. Matthias Alexander and the Reichian mind/bodywork systems that have evolved out of the work of Wilhelm Reich, have emerged from this research and are being used all over the world. All of these techniques, devoted to improving both our sense of well-being and how we function, have had to turn much of their attention to breathing. This mirrors the findings of more ancient systems like Yoga and Qi Gong from India and China, in which breathing techniques played an integral part.

As the air we breathe in becomes more and more crowded with substances other than naturally occurring gases, and as modern working practices demand that our bodies are placed in unfamiliar positions for hours on end, greater attention is being given to how we breathe and the impact our breathing habits have on our lives. Once one looks at improving how any person feels or performs, breathing soon becomes the dominant focus of attention.

STEVE'S STORY

Steve came to see me only because his girlfriend had made the appointment and driven him to my clinic. He was a successful footballer with a promising career ahead of him – at least that is how it had seemed until the panic attacks had begun. As a result of these attacks Steve had begun to drink more heavily than usual and his game was being affected. His coach had begun 'making noises' so Steve went to see his doctor who had offered him a fairly common anti-depressant that sometimes works well in arresting panic attacks. This medication, however, was not without its side effects and it was at this point that his girlfriend, already a Yoga student of mine, made an appointment for Steve to see me. He was clearly embarrassed by what was happening to him.

I observed Steve's breathing while he sat, walked, ran and rested. Then we discussed what had gone wrong to cause his mind and body to stand in the way of his ambitions for himself.

Steve's problem was the direct result of a particularly poor breathing habit, and as we follow his story we will unravel the mystery of how it caused the precise symptoms it did in him. Poor breathing habits can cause muscle cramps and spasms, feelings ranging from vague tiredness to constant exhaustion and general malaise, headaches, extreme pre-menstrual syndrome in women, depression and anxiety, palpitations and chest pains, to name just a few. What happened to Steve has happened to many of us faced with a rapidly changing world that we respond to in old and inappropriate ways. When any threat – real or imaginary – is perceived our bodies reach into our ancient past to deal with these new and modern situations. We need to learn how to adapt and deal with these new conditions much more creatively.

We have to begin by understanding what happens to us when we breathe, and when that breathing changes what our physiological and psychological responses are. Then we can embark on the exciting and revealing journey of observing our own breathing habits and discovering how much they reveal about ourselves.

In the months that followed we investigated and corrected Steve's breathing habits and used parts of a number of the techniques to slowly change those habits until the panic attacks

receded and finally stopped. During these sessions I explained to him the relationship between our world and our breath, our way of breathing and what it discloses about who we are. What follows is the human story as I told it to Steve – a view of life through the prism of the breath.

FROM THERE TO HERE: THE GIFT OF OXYGEN

All living things on this planet are highly organized and extraordinarily complex. The earliest life forms that appeared, probably about 3,500 million years ago, were apparently simple plant-like blue-green algae. However the process that brought them into being, and from which all other life evolved, was anything but simple. To acknowledge in full the miracle of human life is to celebrate complexity – long may that complexity live in order that we may continue to evolve.

THE SPARK

Science tells us that our planet has been around for about 4,500 million years. Initially too hot and dangerous to support any life, it was bombarded by meteors from the forming solar system and ripped apart by violent volcanic explosions being forced up from its own tumultuous depths. This was a heady mix of chemicals that sunlight and lightning would strike. Mother Nature was mixing her soup and some of its ingredients would react with each other. Gradually, over millennia, that reaction produced a simple single-celled being that had the ability to cover itself with some kind of membrane and reproduce itself. The Spark of Life had been lit.

As soon as even these simple life forms appeared on the surface of this planet they began to change its environment. First, photosynthesis began. Light energy from sunlight was converted into chemical energy and slowly 'free' oxygen began to appear.

The atmosphere in which the very first cells had evolved was probably a rather lethal mixture of ammonia, methane and other carbon gases. The new life forms broke down this atmosphere and replaced the deadly methane and ammonia with carbon dioxide and nitrogen. Then more plants evolved creating a new process of photosynthesis which used carbon dioxide as energy and released oxygen into the atmosphere. With the coming of oxygen the stage was set for the appearance of more intricate life forms that would use oxygen as their primary source of energy and release carbon dioxide into the atmosphere. And here we are – breathing beings of infinite variety entirely dependent on each other and the atmosphere we now contribute to creating. Vast forests, acting like the earth's lungs, release oxygen into the atmosphere ready for us to inhale; they also absorb some of the carbon dioxide that we and other breathing beings exhale.

COMING INTO BEING

The way we develop from a simple single cell in the uterus into a complex breathing person made up of trillions of cells retells the story of evolution every time it happens.

As we develop in the watery womb of our mother, we mimic the process of evolution on the planet. From the moment of conception the way is being prepared for the mother to hold within her belly a small ocean giving rise to life that will be nourished through her – just as the vast oceans of the earth nourished that first life on the planet millions of years ago. Through the body of the mother the foetus will be provided with that which the planet provided for the first developing life forms, including oxygen.

The first life on the planet immediately set about changing the environment, and life developing in the uterus will, from the same impulses, transform its habitat in search of the nourishment it needs to evolve and grow. The outer cells of the developing embryo will invade the lining of the womb and embed themselves in it. As the embryo penetrates the tissues of the womb lining it becomes surrounded by ruptured blood vessels and is filled with blood from them. This rich, red blood contains that vital and most precious nutrient: oxygen. Throughout the life of the being in the womb it will receive its oxygen and other nutrients through these blood vessels and use them to dispose of its wastes, including carbon dioxide. The quality of the air it is receiving will depend entirely on its mother. But it is being prepared for an individual and even more complex life.

THE INNER BECOMES THE OUTER

The human being that develops from the embryo is created from three very basic and primitive sets of cells. These are called the mesoderm, the endoderm and the ectoderm cells. Following the basic genetic patterns laid down for them and encoded in their depths, these cells will become muscle, bone, liver, nerve, brain, and so on.

The ectoderm, when the foetus is about two weeks old (usually before most women even know they are pregnant), forms what is called the 'primitive streak'. Then these same cells do something extraordinary. As if using the primitive streak as their marker, they loop and fold themselves on either side of it, enclosing it and creating a groove that will eventually become the neural canal. This canal will form the major communication control centre of the body: the brain and the spinal cord which holds and protects the delicate nerves that carry signals between the body and the brain. This is miraculous enough, but even more remarkable is that in this process of looping and folding the ectoderm has also become the skin, our covering sheath.

Thus the cells which form the very centre of our being also form our most outer self. The internal and the external are not different, not separated, not distinct from each other. Whatever touches the outer self will inform and produce a response from the deep inner self and vice versa. This creates an exquisite sensitivity to our environment which allows us to know exactly where we are and in what kind of atmosphere we find ourselves. This is how we know when it is appropriate to take that first breath.

It also means that our sensitivity to the outer world is exquisite. Every change, however small and insignificant its appearance, will elicit a response and leave an impression – an impression that often changes the way we breathe.

Like all other life on this planet, except for a few simple organisms (some types of bacteria and yeasts), as long as we live we will continue to need oxygen to carry out even the most simple of our life processes. Despite the ways in which our breathing habits might change, the body adapts to these changes and continues to organize itself to get that oxygen from the atmosphere around us.

THE GASES WE BREATHE

The atmosphere of the earth, held here hugging the earth's crust just as we are by the force of gravity, contains many gases. The most plentiful ones are nitrogen, oxygen and carbon dioxide. In fact, nitrogen and oxygen make up about 98 per cent of the air around us. While we need nitrogen we do not absorb it from the air we breathe – we take in our nitrogen from plants. We need oxygen for every bodily process we undergo and the atmosphere at sea-level contains about 21 per cent oxygen. We take in this oxygen with each breath that we breathe.

BREATH IS THE BRIDGE

The next chapter will describe the physiology and anatomy of how we obtain oxygen and release carbon dioxide. What we need to remember is that just as our outer 'shell', the skin, is immediately connected to the deepest and most sensitive part of ourselves, we are also connected via breathing to the atmosphere around us. This passage of air in and out of our bodies will bring us into contact with everything in the atmosphere that has evolved with us.

Every time we breathe in we are breathing in 10^{20} molecules, and every time we breathe out we exhale 10^{20} molecules – that's billions and billions of molecules with each breath. Not all of them are the gases we know are circulating in the environment, such as nitrogen, oxygen, etc. Some of those molecules are bacteria and viruses that our immune systems will have to respond to vigorously if they penetrate our bodies. Many of those molecules will be the molecules that others have breathed out – parts of themselves, their lungs, their livers, their hearts. In this way, once we have been in a room with a group of people for say a dinner party, by the end of the evening we have shared much more than good food and lively conversation. We go home carrying part of them in ourselves. And because this atmosphere is the same one that has been here from the beginning of time, we are connected via the breath to all the breathing beings that ever walked or crawled on this planet.

With this information in mind some smart statisticians have come up with the theory that each of us now carries within us molecules of Christ, the Buddha, the Prophet Mohammed, etc. – all embraced via the breath. Of course, it also means we carry the molecules of Hitler, Genghis Khan and the Caesars. Nothing is excluded.

The stranger passing in the street charged with tension or the loved one in pain, whether physical or emotional, will almost certainly impact on us. The baby who is touched by her/his mother when she herself is feeling tired, frustrated or angry will pick up that message even though the mother is not aware she is signalling her feelings. Parents who find themselves unable to touch and cuddle their children lovingly because of their own background will be signalling their isolation. The breath, touching our inner being as it does, is an open passage for those signals. Most of the time this impact goes unnoticed until something goes wrong, something like panic attacks or chronic fatigue.

By learning to evaluate the way we are breathing we learn just how much the world, its people and places, have impacted on us and how we can use the breath to transform our lives.

A BRIEF HISTORY OF BREATHWORK

My own exploration of breathing began after I met the Himalayan monk who was to become my teacher and spiritual guide. I was in a deep personal crisis when we met and perhaps it takes acute situations to make us realize we have chronic problems. Over the twelve years that I knew Swami Venkatesananda he personally taught me how to become aware of my breathing and how I could use it to change my response to any situation I found myself in – no matter how critical or difficult the situation. Like any true and good guide he held up a mirror in which I could see myself and, of course, what first came to view was something so ghastly that my impulse was to look away. But he encouraged me – in the true sense of that word – he filled me with the courage I needed to keep looking; and he always reminded me that there was a shining sacred self within waiting to be discovered and that the means to it was through the breath.

Swami Venkatesananda taught me the wisdom of breathing using the ancient Yoga techniques of India. In Yoga, whether doing the physical movements that constitute Hatha Yoga, the devotional chanting that is the expression of Bhakti Yoga, or Dhyana Yoga that encompasses meditation, awareness of breath is critical. As a Yoga teacher and therapist I have continued to teach and pass on these techniques.

I only fully appreciated the wonder of these teachings long after Swami Venkatesananda had died, when I studied other kinds of bodywork besides Yoga – I also became an acupuncturist, massage therapist and herbalist. Gradually the truth came to be realized: that breath is pivotal to both our physical well-being and our pathway to freedom, and it is the place where all healing paradigms, from modern technological medicine to the most esoteric and ancient medical systems, converge.

THE DISCOVERERS OF RESPIRATION

Science at its best is without dogma. Nature reveals itself to the scientist through his or her observation. But that revelation is never complete or given all at once – nature seems to reveal herself rather reluctantly. This means that new ideas and new concepts are continually replacing old ones. This is as true in the discovery of how and what we breathe in and out as in any other field of biology or science. Scientists were always interested in where we got our nourishment from, and until some important discoveries about respiration were made, they believed that all life processes were sustained by the food we extracted from the soil and ate. Then nature revealed a bit more of herself and respiration began to make itself known. That nature chose to make this revelation through plant life is interesting.

About three hundred years ago a Belgian physician planted a willow tree in a pot and added only water to its soil from time

to time. At the end of five years he observed that while the willow had gained an impressive 164lbs in weight, the soil in the pot had decreased in weight by only 2 ounces. On the basis of this measurement Monsieur Jan Baptista von Helmont declared that it was the water and not soil that had provided the plant with its substance.

Then on the 17th August 1771, an English clergyman by the name of Joseph Priestley began an experiment involving fire and a sprig of mint. He burnt a candle in the atmosphere inside a container until it became extinguished. We now know that a candle burns out once it has used up all the oxygen available in the atmosphere, but the Reverend Priestley knew no such thing. Once the candle had burnt out he placed his sprig of mint in this atmosphere and noted by the 27th August that 'another candle could be burnt in this same air'. Priestley believed that the sprig of mint had restored the air and that he had hit on a way of restoring air that 'had been injured by the burning of candles'. He was presented with a medal for his work, the citation on which read:

> For whose discoveries we are assured that no vegetable grows in vain . . . but cleanses and purifies our atmosphere.

Other scientists would add to and refine Priestley's original experiment. It was the great French scientist Lavoisier who finally discovered that we breathe in oxygen and produce and breathe out carbon dioxide. Unfortunately the French did not have the same appreciation for Monsieur Lavoisier's work as the English did for the Reverend Priestley's and on the 8th of May, 1794, this scientific genius was guillotined. But 'you can't stop progress' – as my grandmother used to say each time she added a new piece of technology to her kitchen. Again other scientists took up the work of Lavoisier and it was another

Frenchman, Nicholas de Saussure, who demonstrated that plants exchange equal amounts of carbon dioxide for oxygen in the presence of sunlight.

Thus, photosynthesis was finally on the table and, as we shall see photosynthesis is human respiration in reverse. We breathe in oxygen and breathe out carbon dioxide. The great Lavoisier had given the name oxygen to this 'gas of life' – and indeed it is: we live in the presence of oxygen, we heal and repair ourselves in the presence of oxygen and when cells are deprived of oxygen they become damaged and die. This discovery led to an explosion of interest in the part breathing plays in our well-being which began late in the last century and carried on into this one.

THE BREATHWORKERS

In the second half of the nineteenth century a French singing student in Paris, Francois Delsarte, lost his voice – apparently through poor vocal instruction. He turned to exploring his breathing and his movement. A system of movement, in which breathwork was essential, emerged from his self-study. This system was adopted and taken to America by one of his students, Steele Mackay, where it became extremely popular and where others learned and taught its methods. Most of these teachers would evolve their own method out of the original Delsarte system. In the early 1900s it returned to Europe via Germany where a bodywork system known as *Gymnastik* had begun. Two of the great breathing teachers of this system were a German, Hede Kallmeyer, and an American living in Hamburg, Bess Mesendieck. Breathing teachers like Elsa Gindler emerged from the *Gymnastik* system and others taught by her, like the famous American teacher Carola Speads, are still teaching. Another famous breathing teacher to come from this period who is still teaching is the German, Ilsa Middendorf.

While these systems of breathwork are easily accessible in Germany, Holland, France and the USA, their popularity never reached England. Most recently the breathwork teacher who has created the greatest controversy is the Russian physician, Professor Konstantin Buteyko, whose method is applied specifically to people suffering from asthma – although he claims it works equally well on high blood pressure and a number of other disorders.

In most of the United Kingdom it is in Yoga, Chi Gong and Tai Chi classes, or through systems like the Alexander Technique, that the vast majority of people will first encounter their breathing habits and begin to learn to change them. Only occasionally will a doctor refer people to be taught breathing and then it will be via a psychotherapist or physiotherapist. Physicians who are focusing on the link between habits of breathing and physical well-being, are a relatively recent phenomenon still in the minority.

What is clear to any bodyworker, however, is that no healing system can overlook breathwork. The failure of modern medicine to do so with more focus is serious. Few GPs will advise asthma sufferers, emphysema patients or depressed or anxious patients, to seek advice on breathing. Sadly, fewer still will themselves have any education in being able to help their patients review and change their breathing habits. Often their dismissal of systems that do pay attention to breathwork will erode the patient's confidence in seeking out help from sources outside of the medical profession. When Steve told his GP that he was learning to breathe with me, his GP dismissed it with a gesture and muttered something about 'mumbo jumbo and quacks taking your money'. Fortunately for Steve by then he was experiencing the benefit of the work we were doing together.

We, as breathers, need to take note of what doctors like Phillip James MD, PhD, CHB, DIH, FFOM are saying. I list his

professional credentials here to illustrate that he is making his criticism from inside the medical profession. Dr James writes that, 'Medical students are taught little about oxygen and can only remember that it can be toxic in excess.'[1]

SPIRITUS

When considering breathwork we span a whole spectrum of healing approaches, from the ancient to the modern, from the rational to the metaphysical, because breath is integral to all of them. It expands beyond the boundaries of healing systems into spiritual disciplines, taking seekers into what the poet Rumi called 'the breath inside the breath'.

Therein lies the true miracle of breathwork: it not only improves physical functioning but acts as a pathway inward to the self, because breath is the bridge between body and mind and between mind and spirit. To the Yogis it is the life-force and vitality of all beings. To the Romans the word for breath was *spiritus* which also meant spirit, and it is the common root found in respiration, inspiration and aspiration. To the ancient Greeks breath, wind and soul were all said to be the same.

1. Philip James PhD, FFOM. Hyperbaric Oxygen Therapy and Multiple Sclerosis: Where Are We Now? *The Lancet*, 13 February 1992.

CONTRACTION AND EXPANSION

Internal respiration . . . establishes the integrity of each cell and its relationship to its internal, fluid environment. External respiration or lung breathing . . . establishes our own personal separateness and our relationship to our external air environment.

BERYL BAINBRIDGE

As we have seen in the previous chapter, our evolution designed us so that, in the most economical way possible, we obtain oxygen from our environment to create the energy that powers the entire body. Breathing happens by our super-sensitivity to our environment and by the natural laws that govern everything on this planet. To understand how we breathe we have to understand how air, made up of oxygen, carbon dioxide and a number of other gases, behave in the natural world.

AIR UNDER PRESSURE

All gases follow a simple rule – they move from an area of high pressure to an area of low pressure. Apart from our breathing, this rule impacts our everyday life in a number of ways. For example, we are relying on this behaviour of gas every time we fill the tyres on our car. At the garage you attach a line from an air compressor to a small nozzle in your tyre. As soon as you squeeze the lever you hear the hissing air enter your tyre and it begins to inflate. When the air in your tyre has reached the necessary pressure you release the lever and the flow of air is blocked off. The tyre does not have to do anything to cause the air to enter it – the air (made up of various gases) simply moves in a way that is natural to it: flowing from an area of high pressure (the compressor) to an area of low pressure (your tyre). Children have no understanding of the rules and natural laws of gases but they know how to pump up their bicycle tyres using a small hand-held air compressor. As they pump away at the compressor with their hands, air in the tube is compressed and then flows from that high pressure to the tyre where it is at low pressure.

It is this rule that makes our bodies breathe. The air in the atmosphere, being pulled down by gravity just as we are, exerts a certain pressure. Our chest cavity, in which our lungs are situated, is called the thoracic cavity. When we have exhaled, the pressure in the thoracic cavity and the pressure in the earth's atmosphere are equal. Then some powerful muscles spring into action to lift and expand the ribs and cause the floor of the thoracic cavity to descend, expanding the space. As space is made in the thoracic cavity the air already in it is under less pressure than the air in the atmosphere outside, so air simply flows in and we experience this in-flow as an inhalation. The body is a highly intelligent pressure gauge and as soon as enough air has entered, the muscles begin to release – the ribs relax back down and the floor of the thoracic cavity lifts. This diminishing space means the air in the thoracic cavity comes under greater pressure than the air outside so the air flows out and we experience that outflow as an exhalation.

The powerful diaphragm muscle is our most important breathing muscle. It is its descent and ascent that changes the space for the earth's atmosphere to flow into and out of our bodies.

Imagine a bottle with a cork in the top and that you have attached a balloon to the inside end of this cork. Instead of a glass bottom this bottle has a rubber bottom.

Let us assume that the pressure inside the bottle is the same as outside, so if you pierced the cork and made a hole in it nothing would happen: the balloon would neither inflate nor deflate. However, if you then pull the rubber bottom of the bottle downward you will have made more space – and therefore less pressure – on the inside of the bottle. This extra space which lowers the air pressure in the bottle will cause air from the outside to flow in through the hole in the cork and inflate the balloon. As you release your hold on the rubber, the pressure in the bottle will increase in relation to the air outside the bottle so the air will flow out of the hole and the balloon will deflate.

Figure 1: When you pull down the rubber bottom of the jar you create more space within it and therefore a lower atmospheric pressure – air then rushes in. If you release the rubber bottom the air pressure outside the jar will be less than inside the jar and the air will rush out, deflating the balloon.

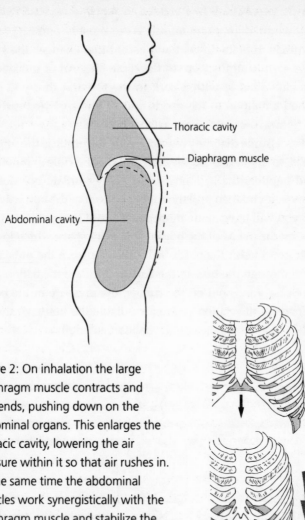

Thoracic cavity

Diaphragm muscle

Abdominal cavity

Figure 2: On inhalation the large
diaphragm muscle contracts and
descends, pushing down on the
abdominal organs. This enlarges the
thoracic cavity, lowering the air
pressure within it so that air rushes in.
At the same time the abdominal
muscles work synergistically with the
diaphragm muscle and stabilize the
abdominal organs. When you breathe
out the diaphragm relaxes and returns
upward to its wonderful dome shape.
This decreases the air pressure in the
thoracic cavity and air flows out.

PRINCIPLES OF BREATHWORK

That is exactly how we breathe. Once we have exhaled an ordinary breath the pressure in our bodies and in the outside atmosphere are equal and there is no movement of air. Then your body tugs at the powerful diaphragm muscle which acts as the 'bottom' of the thoracic cavity of the body.

The diaphragm muscle begins to descend, creating more space in the thoracic cavity – and therefore less pressure than outside – and air rushes in through the nose and throat to enter the lungs which expand with the thorax. At a certain point the diaphragm muscle stops its descent and begins to ascend, and as it does so the lungs begin to contract. As the space in the thorax decreases, the air in the lungs is under higher pressure than the air outside so it leaves the same way it entered, through the nose or mouth.

PARTIAL PRESSURE

The pressure the whole atmosphere exerts is made up of the combined pressures of each of the individual gases that exist within it. At the same time each individual gas produces its own pressure – this can be measured and it is called *partial pressure*. The partial pressure of any gas is dependent on the number of molecules of that particular gas in a mixture. For example, you can measure the partial pressure of oxygen in the atmosphere separately from the partial pressure of carbon dioxide.

We can also do these measurements in the human body. Both oxygen and carbon dioxide travel through the lungs to and from every part of our body via the arteries and veins entering and leaving tissue cells. At every stage we can measure the partial pressure of either of these gases in any one of these places: in the alveoli of the lungs, in the arteries, or in the veins. This concept of partial pressure is very important to understanding how we take in the oxygen we need, how

our body controls our rate of breathing, and how we expel carbon dioxide.

For instance, when the gas mixture of the atmosphere has been inhaled into the lungs, the partial pressure of oxygen in the air which is taken into the lungs is greater than the partial pressure of oxygen in the blood flowing to the lungs. This is because the blood returning from its journey through the body is carrying mostly carbon dioxide which it collected while it was depositing oxygen. Following the natural law for gas, oxygen will then flow down the pressure gradient, entering the blood from the lungs until the partial pressure of oxygen in the blood is equal to the partial pressure of oxygen in the lungs.

Carbon dioxide will act in exactly the same way, only going the other way. Thus there will be more carbon dioxide in the blood flowing to the lungs than in the air which has just been breathed into the lungs, so the partial pressure of the carbon dioxide in the blood will be greater than in the lungs. Therefore carbon dioxide will flow down the pressure gradient, leaving the blood to enter the air in the lungs which we will breathe out.

This whole exchange of oxygen and carbon dioxide is called *respiration*. Our first contact with our atmosphere is against our skin. Next we inhale it into our lungs. Our blood picks up the vital oxygen we need from the air in the lungs and carries it through the body, delivering it to our cells via the arteries. While depositing this oxygen it picks up carbon dioxide to transport back to the lungs via the veins. We then breathe out the carbon dioxide that has been delivered to the lungs, infusing the atmosphere with ourselves.

EXTERNAL AND INTERNAL RESPIRATION

Inhaling into the lungs and exhaling out of them is called *external* respiration, and the complex and wonderful system involved in it is called the respiratory system. Muscles, primarily the diaphragm muscle, but also some powerful secondary muscles, expand the body to create the condition for air to flow into the lungs and then as these muscles relax and return to their resting length, the body contracts and the air flows out. In that space of time an exchange of gases has taken place: we have exchanged carbon dioxide for oxygen.

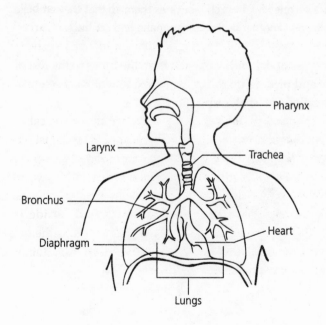

Figure 3: The Respiratory System

Inhalation and exhalation usually take place through the nose. The nasal cavities are designed with hairs and cilia which trap dust and other foreign particles. From the nostrils the air goes to the *pharynx* (back of the throat), from there to the *larynx* (upper throat) and *trachea* (throat). The trachea splits into two branches called the *bronchioles*. The bronchioles end in *alveoli,* which are minute air sacs clustered like bunches of grapes at the end of the bronchioles. It is actually in the alveoli that the exchange of gas takes place between the air in the lungs and the blood. A pair of human lungs have about 300 million alveoli – this provides a surface area for gas exchange of about 750 sq. feet – 40 times the surface area of your body. The wonderful sponginess of the lungs makes them an ideal environment for this exchange. The lungs themselves are surrounded by a membrane, as are the walls of the thoracic cavity, known as the pleura. This pleura secretes fluid which lubricates them so that they are able to slide past one another as the lungs expand and contract.

The process of delivering oxygen from the lungs to the rest of the body and picking up the carbon dioxide that has been produced is called 'internal' respiration.

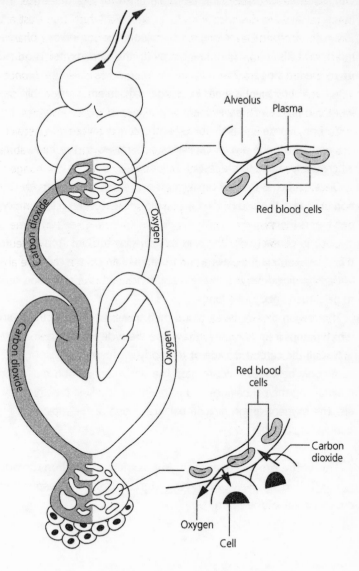

Figure 4: Internal Respiration

Oxygen-laden air enters the lungs and carbon dioxide leaves the lungs.

Oxygen from the alveoli enters the blood. It is carried by both the red blood cells and by plasma – but by far the most oxygen is picked up by the red blood cells.

In the alveoli there is a gas exchange: oxygen enters the capillaries while carbon dioxide leaves them.

Carbon dioxide leaves the blood and enters the alveoli.

Blood leaves the alveoli capillaries and travels to the heart from where it is pumped to the rest of the body.

Once it reaches the tiny capillaries it exchanges the oxygen for carbon dioxide in the body cells. Carbon dioxide leaves the cells and oxygen enters them.

Once in contact with the cells oxygen disassociates from the red blood cells, enters the plasma and from there enters the cells.

Carbon dioxide leaves the cells and binds with the red blood cells to be carried back to the lungs.

The carbon dioxide-laden blood then travels back up to the heart which pumps it up into the lungs where the cycle repeats itself.

Not all the carbon dioxide of the body is expelled – it is not, as is commonly believed, a waste gas. The body uses carbon dioxide in maintaining the pH balance and to maintain or adjust breathing levels. The oxygen/carbon dioxide balance is one of the most vital for human functioning.

This entire process of exchanging oxygen and carbon dioxide is controlled by nerves carrying signals from the respiration control areas of the brain.

The body will always and in all circumstances seek balance. This balance is called homeostasis. An American physiologist called Walter Cannon who spoke of 'the wisdom of the body' was the first to use the term homeostasis to describe our ability to maintain stable internal conditions in a constantly and often wildly changing environment.

When you think that we are made up of trillions of cells, all in a state of unceasing activity, you realize how wonderful this balancing mechanism is. It also makes you realize that the body is nothing like a machine. A machine stops if the smallest thing goes wrong: a screw becoming loose or a bit of grit in a single part. Our bodies, on the other hand, working always towards balance, make extraordinary adjustments before things go so far out of balance as to produce problems. Homeostasis applies as much to breathing as it does to any other biological system. Breathing can and does affect our fine balancing mechanisms in many of the body's activities.

METABOLISM

Our body uses energy on a grand scale. Every cell is involved in the process of using energy to extract more energy, from air and food and then this energy is used to drive every body system and every move we make. Most of this energy comes from burning (breaking down) carbohydrates in the presence of oxygen. This produces (building up) energy, carbon dioxide and water. This process of transformation that involves building up and breaking down is called *metabolism*. This is the reverse of the photosynthesis we looked at in Chapter One: plants, in the presence of sunlight, breathe in carbon dioxide and breathe out oxygen. Animals breathe in oxygen and breathe out carbon dioxide – in or out of the presence of sunlight.

Both the amount of carbohydrate and oxygen used up, and the amount of energy, carbon dioxide and water produced, depends on our energy needs at any given moment. For example, relaxing in front of the television will use less oxygen and produce less carbon dioxide than running for a bus because we use less energy relaxing than running. The body will make the adjustments to our breathing depending on our need for energy throughout the day and night – an evening spent at a nightclub dancing will probably call on more energy than was used sitting in front of a computer at work.

In its constant search for homeostasis our bodies will adjust the breathing to keep the oxygen and carbon dioxide levels safe. You will breathe more deeply when you are running around than when resting. The body will make adjustments to your rate of breathing to ensure that:

- You are taking in enough oxygen for your energy requirements at the time, and
- That the levels of carbon dioxide are maintained at an optimum level.

If, for example, you started 'deep breathing' and were not doing exercise at the time, you would lower the carbon dioxide levels in your body which would create a number of problems.

PH BALANCE

One of the most sensitive balance conditions in our bodies is the acid/alkaline balance of our body fluids, which is called the pH balance. pH is usually measured on a scale of 1 to 14, so that a pH factor of 7 indicates neutrality. Less than 7 indicates acidity and more than 7 alkalinity. The pH level of the blood functions well within the very narrow margins of 7.36 to 7.41. If the pH of the blood rises above 7.45 a person is said to have *alkalosis*, and if it drops below 7.35 they are said to have *acidosis*. Breathing very directly affects the body's pH balance. Because the body uses carbon dioxide and converts it to maintain its acid levels, low carbon dioxide can cause the blood to push towards an alkaline state. One example of this happening is when someone breathes in more oxygen than they are converting to carbon dioxide. The low carbon dioxide level causes a condition known as *respiratory alkalosis*. Respiratory acidosis occurs when, through an illness the person is breathing in such a way that carbon dioxide levels rise above their acceptable levels, such as pneumonia, emphysema or cystic fibrosis. Respiratory acidosis is most frequently associated with an illness that affects the lungs while respiratory alkalosis is usually associated with poor breathing habits.

The panic attacks Steve was suffering from had their origin **in the balance of the partial pressures of oxygen and carbon dioxide going awry in his system**. His breathing created the condition of *respiratory alkalosis* which set him up for the panic attacks.

Steve was a chronic 'upper chest' breather. His abdomen hardly moved at all when he breathed so that most movement and expansion in his body was in the upper chest. Added to this he almost always breathed through his mouth rather than his nose, and his inhalations lasted longer than his exhalations. These factors combined led to a fall in the partial pressure *of* carbon dioxide in his blood and the alveoli of his lungs, causing an imbalance (or loss of homeostasis) in his pH levels. In respiratory alkalosis the blood vessels to the brain constrict, reducing the flow of blood. The change is minute but the effect is literally breathtaking!

You may have seen people gasping for breath in what is called a hyperventilation attack or you yourself may have had such an attack. While they keep gasping, feeling they cannot get a full breath, what they in fact need is less breath: <u>less</u> oxygen and <u>more</u> carbon dioxide. That is why the common remedy is to give them a paper bag to breathe into. This enables them to breathe back some of the carbon dioxide they have just breathed out and slowly the system returns to normal. Hyperventilation is what Steve was doing all the time – taking in more oxygen than he could convert to carbon dioxide and more oxygen than he required for his metabolic needs. When this upset the balance of oxygen to carbon dioxide enough it had a knock-on effect on the pH balance until eventually the body produced a panic attack.

Low carbon dioxide levels create a condition akin to acute stress. Why should hyperventilation produce panic attacks? Why should it produce chronic fatigue, muscle cramps and spasms, chest pains, pre-menstrual syndrome, palpitations, cold feet and hands even on warm days, dizziness, dry mouth and throat, acid regurgitation, heartburn, flatulence, belching, feelings of depersonalization, impaired concentration, impaired memory, disturbed sleep and even allergies? Remember, your body is working towards balance: if you have a habit that constantly disrupts that balance the body will try to defend itself and part of that defence is the signal it sends to change the status quo. We will see in the next chapter how one physician believes this to be the major cause of asthma.

In any temporary emergency our body interrupts its basic metabolic rhythms to deal with the situation. For example, if your burglar alarm goes off in the middle of the night your body will instantly stall normal functioning to help you deal with a possible threat from outside – and it will do so *in anticipation*. Before you know for sure there is an intruder your body will be on full alert. You will notice some of the changes: your mouth will go dry and your breathing will become more shallow and rapid as the muscles in your lower abdomen and pelvic floor tense for action. What will also be happening is that the blood will be drawn away from the processes of digestion and elimination and sent to the extremities, the legs and arms, to give you the energy you need to either turn and run or stand and fight: commonly called the flight or fight response. If you are a chronic hyperventilator your nervous system has been on this kind of full alert for so long that stress has become a chronic condition and the normal 'housekeeping' functions of the body are subdued while this stress is maintained.

The nervous system of the body is divided into the *central nervous system* and the *autonomic nervous system.* In fact there is only one nervous system but we divide it up only to understand its different functioning parts. The central nervous system controls our muscular responses and voluntary movements. It is the central nervous system that takes us out on the date we want to go on. The autonomic nervous system controls all our involuntary functions like our heartbeat, liver and kidney functions, metabolic rate, pH balance, etc. The autonomic nervous system, in other words, keeps us alive while we are out on that date.

The autonomic nervous system is further divided into two: the sympathetic nervous system and the parasympathetic

nervous system and it is these that should keep us balanced between extreme anxiety and functional calm. They are best illustrated with a diagram. The important thing to remember is that breathing is under the control of both the central nervous system and the autonomic nervous system. In other words it is both in our control and out of our control. You can hold your breath but if you hold it too long you will faint and your body will breathe as soon as you lose consciousness. Breath is also the bridge between the sympathetic nervous system (which excites) and the parasympathetic nervous system (which calms).

CHRONIC FATIGUE

If an incident like the burglar alarm happens the sympathetic nervous system is on full alert. Once you have discovered that the alarm was set off by your cat and not an intruder intent on harm, you will want to go back to sleep but may feel 'wired'. This is because the sympathetic nervous system has been triggered. To activate the parasympathetic nervous system you can use calming, full awareness breathing techniques. But what happens when the sympathetic nervous system is switched on and left on? What if after the alarm you tried to go back to sleep immediately but couldn't, became frustrated, then finally fell asleep in the small hours of the morning only to be woken shortly afterwards by a jangling alarm clock telling you it's time to get up? Then you had an argument with your spouse about whose cat it is anyway and who should have put it out. At work there is a general computer failure and the figures you needed for a meeting at three o'clock are not obtainable. You finally get home that evening and the cat is calmly stretched out on your favourite chair but you cannot relax immediately because the baby has to be taken to the doctor because she's throwing up.

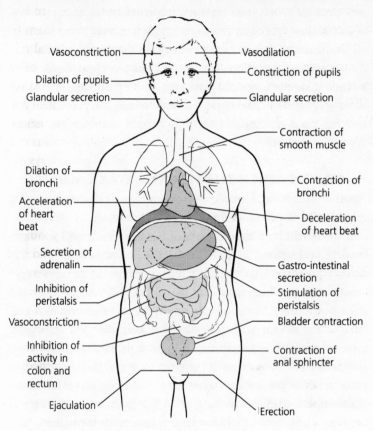

Vasoconstriction ——————— Vasodilation

Dilation of pupils ————— Constriction of pupils

Glandular secretion ——————— Glandular secretion

Contraction of
smooth muscle

Dilation of
bronchi ————

Contraction of
bronchi

Acceleration
of heart
beat ——————

Deceleration
of heart beat

Secretion of
adrenalin ——————

Gastro-intestinal
secretion

Inhibition of
peristalsis ——————

Stimulation of
peristalsis

Vasoconstriction ——————

Bladder contraction

Inhibition of
activity in
colon and
rectum ——————

Contraction of
anal sphincter

Ejaculation ——————

Erection

Figure 5: The Nervous System

In a modern world this is the pattern of most of our lives. As
a supposed break from this norm we take a hectic three week
holiday that usually means mobilizing a whole family and
moving to a strange destination. The body is unable to sustain
this and a constant background fatigue sets. At this stage many
people will start taking vitamins and minerals in an attempt to

perk themselves up, or visit their GPs who will conduct a battery of tests. When their tests are returned and nothing proves negative they feel even worse about themselves, believing it is all 'in the mind'. While I am a believer in diet supplementation, it is a great frustration that more health-care professionals, including doctors, are not educated to help address the most basic and fundamental energy system of the body: breathing – and the poor quality of breathing which underlies so many diverse symptoms.

CHEST PAINS – THE HEART ATTACK MIMIC

Another symptom, chronic muscle cramps and spasms, are a good signal of poor breathing. Even in moderate hyperventilation there will be a loss of carbon dioxide which will increase tension and spasm in muscles as they maintain an attack/defend posture. This can also lead to chest pains and even breathlessness which may lead people to believe they are having a heart attack. Some people might present themselves regularly at the doctor with this disorder and once the tests that indicate cardiovascular dysfunction have proved negative, they are dismissed. On each such occasion they will be bewildered – their tests will not confirm what they know they felt at the time. If attention is paid to breathing just a few moments of a doctor's or nurse's time could yield surprising results for the better.

PRE-MENSTRUAL SYNDROME

Poor breathing habits can greatly exacerbate the symptoms of pre-menstrual syndrome. In the week to ten days before the onset of menstruation a woman's progesterone levels peak, causing carbon dioxide levels in the blood to drop. If the woman is a chronic hyperventilator this drop will be in addition to the lowered level she is already living with and irritability, muscle cramps, headaches and fatigue will result.

The list of conditions poor breathing habits can cause or aggravate is quite extensive. Steve's panic attacks were a direct result of respiratory alkalosis and breathing retraining was the essential treatment. Steve had to learn how to breathe so as to allow for the participation of his diaphragm. This meant learning to soften the abdomen and pelvic floor muscles so that they could welcome the descending diaphragm muscle rather than interfering in its descent. In order for this to happen his whole being had to become involved in observation and intervention.

CONTRACTION, EXPANSION, EQUILIBRIUM

The ancient Yogis of India saw the whole of life as being governed by three forces: expansion, contraction and equilibrium. In Sanskrit, the original language of the Yogis, these are *rajas*, *tamas* and *sattva* respectively. The clearest expression of these forces at work is in our breathing. We breathe in and expand, we breathe out and contract, and after the exhalation there is a brief resting phase where we are neither breathing in nor breathing out which corresponds to the phase of sattva, or equilibrium. Between exhalation and inhalation the pressure both inside and outside of the body is the same and only changes once the body has begun to expand with the descent of the diaphragm.

We function best, the Yogis said, when each of these phases is allowed to fulfill itself and function in harmony with the others. In fact, during the phase of equilibrium when we have breathed out, there is still air left in the lungs. This means that between breaths an exchange of oxygen and carbon dioxide is still going on between the residual air in the alveoli of our lungs and our blood. This process is vital for 'levelling off' the ratio of oxygen to carbon dioxide in the blood.

The body is using all three phases, expansion, contraction and equilibrium, to maintain balance. The very worst thing poor breathing habits do is interfere with one of these phases and therefore with all three. How and why this happens is the subject of most serious mind-bodywork systems.

When the exquisitely sensitive balancing mechanisms of the body are able to maintain stability we experience this stability as a wonderful flow of energy through our entire being and a desire to live and experience life in its fullness. To achieve this we have to:

- learn to relax the abdominal and pelvic floor muscles so that the diaphragm can descend down into the belly,
- release the intercostal muscles so that they can effectively pull the ribs up and away from the hips during inhalation,
- learn to intervene in the tension of muscles that are constraining the breathing process,
- become aware of the tide of air entering and leaving the body, and slow down it down, and
- encourage the return of a full flow of saliva into the mouth.

REORGANIZING EXPERIENCE

Accomplishing this requires reorganizing your body's responses to your life experiences. Steve's life would always have the same pressures as long as he remained a footballer with high ambitions for himself. What had to happen was that he had to learn to take conscious control of what was happening physically as a result of that stress. He then had to intervene in his old habits and learn to bring full attention – without an excess of tension – to his game.

Just as breathing spans many systems of balance and activity in the body, awareness of breathing means awareness of all our

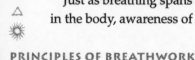

responses throughout the day to the lives we lead. Having taken this step backwards we can look forward at how changing the breathing affects these responses.

TOWARDS FREEDOM

Insanity is doing the same thing over and over again
and expecting a different result.

ALBERT EINSTEIN

Respiration – the contraction and expansion of our thoracic cavity that allows for a free flow of the earth's
atmosphere in and out and through our bodies – relies
on the action of muscles. It is when these muscles become con-
stricted, caught up in habitual tensions, that problems arise
because then the changes in breathing, as we have seen, can
have uncomfortable results. Even the smallest change can have
a cascade effect that will have an enormous impact on the way
we function.

I remember well Alan, an acquaintance who came to me for
treatment some time ago. I had met him on and off at social
gatherings for a number of years. He was 47 years old and
among a new but fast growing breed of computer technocrats;
he smoked upward of 60 cigarettes a day and drank at least a
bottle of wine and a few pints of beer in the same period.
Always the life and soul of the party, unmarried but often with

different pretty women accompanying him, he had a ready wit and apparently easy manner with people. He had mentioned once when he found out that I was an acupuncturist and herbalist that he suffered from mild Raynaud's Syndrome, a condition in which the blood supply to the hands and feet is restricted, leaving them cold and often red or purple looking. I think I gave him my card and said he should phone for an appointment but I did not hear from him immediately.

Then one day much later he did phone. When he came for an appointment he explained that he had developed a leg ulcer that was not only not responding to treatment, it was getting bigger. His doctor, clearly a man who did not believe in pulling his punches, had warned him that his lifestyle of excess combined with very little exercise had severely compromised his circulation and that unless he stopped smoking he could be looking at amputation before he reached 60. He wanted to know if, as an acupuncturist, I could 'stick a few needles in' to stop him smoking.

I gave him a large, hot ayurvedic tea containing cinnamon and black pepper, which are good for circulation, and while he sipped it grimacing I told him that acupuncture had never stopped anyone from smoking – that if *he* stopped smoking acupuncture could act as an aid but that was all. Alan looked frustrated. I suggested that as a way towards giving up smoking we could work together on his breathing habits and that this might also help his circulation. Although he agreed, I knew it was out of desperation and that he was not going to be the most enthusiastic patient I had ever had.

When I put my hands on Alan I was immediately aware that his breathing was barely perceptible. It was as if his body was playing dead. The muscles between the ribs had tightened to the extent that they hardly moved and the wonderful, natural mobility of the diaphragm muscle was almost entirely inhibited

by rigidity in his abdomen and lower back. There was only the slightest movement in his belly to show that he was actually breathing. It was the direct opposite of watching a baby breathe where the entire abdomen, chest and back expand and contract with the breath. Alan's body was playing dead.

To discover what had happened to Alan we need to look more closely at muscle participation during breathing.

Between breaths, during the equilibrium stage, the diaphragm muscle rests briefly. Then, at a signal from the nervous system, two bands of connective tissue called *crura* which are attached to the upper three or four lumbar vertebrae and the diaphragm muscle, make a tug. This causes the diaphragm muscle to descend, gently pushing down against the abdominal organs and intestines and making the belly go out. At the same time muscles between the ribs (the intercostal muscles) pull the ribs up and away from the hips. At another signal these muscles begin to relax and return to their resting positions, which for the diaphragm is its unique dome shape.

In a relaxed body – like that of a baby – this expansion and contraction is easily visible to any observer. You can see by this that full and complete breathing is not dependent on the lungs but entirely on particular muscles. However, the truth about muscle is that there are not really different muscles in our body. That naming and differentiation is for clinical purposes only. If something goes wrong with one muscle this will have a wave effect through the whole musculature of the body. One breath-worker, Gay Hendricks, in his excellent book *Conscious Breathing* (see Resources), gives a quote from Michael Grant White, a breathwork teacher:

> Your shoulder muscles can restrict your breathing. Your chest muscles can restrict your breathing. Your ankle muscles can restrict your breathing.

Many other muscles need to work in concert with the diaphragm and intercostals to achieve full respiration.

A number of muscles in the back, which act primarily as postural muscles, play an important role in breathing – for example, stabilizing the bottom rib for inhalation or forced exhalation, as in a sneeze or cough. Sustained contraction or chronic tension of any of these will compromise the breathing in general.

Many muscles not directly involved with breathing can inhibit the process of breathing. What happens to us as we reach adulthood is that other muscles have gone into a chronic state of tension and contraction, preventing the diaphragm muscle from fully descending and therefore inhibiting the movement of the ribs.

TIGHTENING INWARD

Muscles can become restricted for a number of reasons: poor posture, accidents like falling or bumping into things. However, most of our muscle restrictions are the result of an habitual action we have set up in our bodies in response to the lives we live. Alan's body was a remarkable testimony to muscles tightening to protect the person they had come into being to serve.

One of the great systems of bodywork developed in India over several millennia was Yoga. Yoga, as we saw in the last chapter, pays tribute to the three forces of expansion, contraction and equilibrium. You may have been to a Yoga class or seen the classical Yoga postures being done. Yoga has been thought of in the West as a form of exercise – one of the Yoga associations in Britain is even under the umbrella of the Sports Council. However, by its very nature, exercise is all about increasing power and control. In its history in India, Yoga was never an exercise – it was devised as a means of achieving

grace, ease and fluidity in movement and increased energy through the harmony of the three forces of expansion, contraction and equilibrium. The Yoga postures, therefore, far from being exercises for power and control, are about releasing, lengthening, letting go. This is because Yoga recognized that the chronic state of tension in an adult body was one of contraction – tightening inward.

No system comparable to Yoga was developed in the West until this century. Then a great revolutionary spirit was born, Wilhelm Reich. I have always thought of him as some old Yogi soul born again to take another look at the body, how it breathes and how that breathing impacts on our well-being.

Reich, whose work with respiration and sexual dysfunction led to the advent of several body-based psychotherapies, was the first person to speak of 'muscle armouring'. Blocked breathing, to Reich, was essentially caused by this muscle armouring. He maintained that, in response to the environment, the free and uninhibited breathing of a baby is gradually eroded. The baby, exquisitely sensitive to its world, sensing internal needs that it has to suppress because of the responses their expression evokes in the carers around it, begins to tighten muscles – primarily the diaphragm muscle. This tightening will then continue to the pelvis, chest, back, legs and throat as the baby resists its own natural impulses that evoke hostile responses from its environment. The baby begins to learn how to hold back – and as this process continues the tension in the muscles becomes set and the muscle can be said to be 'armoured'. The muscle never returns spontaneously to its original resting state but remains rigid and drawn in.

Of course, it is not just babies who do this. We adults do it all the time, habituated to it from childhood. When we are involved in a situation where we feel unable to express how we really feel we will tighten our jaw, lock our tongue to the roof of our mouth and tighten our throat. We even have language which describes it, 'I bit back my tears/anger/disappointment.' Do this often enough and these muscles will hold this tension and eventually become exactly what Reich described as armoured muscle. Thus the process of expansion, contraction and equilibrium is compromised. Sometimes it is not so compromised as to cause problems that demand our attention – but certainly enough so that we never feel fully satisfied, fully breathed, and there will just be the occasional nagging headache and background fatigue. Sometimes it is compromised enough to cause extreme symptoms as it did with Steve and Alan, where their functioning was being interrupted.

THE LANGUAGE OF THE BODY
AND THOSE WHO UNDERSTAND IT

In his book *Character Analysis* Reich speaks about the body as being our first and primary communicator. In a chapter with the wonderful title, The Expressive Language of the Living, he reminds us that human speech is a form of expression 'at an advanced stage of development' and that this is true both individually and in an evolutionary sense. Long before language existed our bodies were communicating what we felt. How this is often at odds with what we are expressing was very well demonstrated by Alan's situation.

To overcome muscle armouring and inward contraction, the very first thing that has to be addressed is the chronic holding patterns of the abdominal and pelvic floor muscles. All Reichian methods – including Bioenergetics developed by Alexander Lowen – focus on releasing body tension and returning one to full and creative breathing. Alexander Lowen was a student of Reich, and his bodywork system, Bioenergetics, is based on the work of Reich. In the words of Lowen, 'Bioenergetics is a therapeutic technique to help a person get back together with

42   his body and to help him enjoy to the fullest degree possible the
life of the body.'

It is essential in these techniques that a therapist is present, as
the return to deep abdominal breathing requires the release of
blocked emotions through the expression of these emotions.
The therapist places the person in postures that will provoke
tension and bring to the surface whatever emotion caused the
muscles to become inhibited initially, and then encourages the
full release of that emotion in the therapy session.

The Alexander Technique – named after the man who developed it, an Australian actor F. Matthias Alexander – takes a different approach. After Alexander had suffered from a loss of
voice which the medical profession was unable to help him
with, he began a long process of self-examination and transformation which he then taught to others. His technique became
popular and respected all over the world and is used by people
in and out of the medical profession to transform what he
called 'their use of themselves'.

Our primary instrument is our body – we direct it to move in
this world to accomplish all that we wish to accomplish.
Alexander spent a number of years critically watching how his
use of his own body stood in the way of his full use of voice.
What he learned liberated his voice and his breathing (it is
impossible to liberate one without the other), and he gave up
acting as more and more people clamoured to learn from him
what he had taught himself. Alexander showed great belief in
the human spirit that functioned within the physical frame – he
knew that all people wanted to function to their maximum
capacity and could, provided they received the guidance that
would release them from the chains of old habits. He remarked
to one of his students about breathing, 'This isn't breathing; it is
lifting your chest and collapsing.'

In order to breathe and move more freely, with more poise

and grace, Alexander said change was necessary – and that 'Change involves carrying out an activity against the habit of a lifetime.'

This is as true for breathing as it is for any other activity we use our bodies for. The Alexander Technique insists it is not a therapy but a technique that can be taught. A teacher of the technique will take a student through a number of everyday tasks: sitting, standing, walking, lying down and, of course, breathing, guiding him or her in learning how to intervene in the habits of stress to arrive at a better use of themselves. Through practice on everyday tasks these new habits become embedded and can then be carried over into more complex tasks and situations.

Yoga is also different from therapist-based systems. Like the Alexander Technique, Yoga requires the presence of a teacher to give the student the option of moving in a different direction. The teacher gives guidance until the student fully understands the direction, but from then on it is essential that the process is carried out on your own and on a regular basis. This is partly because the process immediately involves conscious breathing as a means of release, not only as a result. Yoga also does not require the full recall of any of the emotions that may have provoked a life-long habit of tension. To the Yogi, the tightened, tense muscle is the body's way of remembering the trauma, and restoring that muscle to its resting length is the complete release.

My impression when I placed my hands on Alan's body was of fear frozen and turned inward. Yet this was certainly not how someone meeting him in a social setting would have described him, considering his genial conversation and ready banter. As Reich had observed, what his body was saying and what he was verbalizing were not the same thing. Alan had spent all of his life contracting inwards, retreating, locking his

greatest potential deep enough for no-one to reach. As we continue with his story in the next chapter you will see how this was a wise and life-sustaining organization of himself. He was threatened and so hid the very best of himself far enough inside to protect it. Unfortunately that had become a habit that had continued long after the threat had been removed. His life spark had been hidden for so long that even he had forgotten about its existence. Only a crisis led him to unlock what was hidden and allow it to emerge. In the words of the song and the movie, Alan had been '. . . waiting to exhale'.

Muscle, acting as an ally, had tightened to protect the whole. The point at which that tightening had itself become threatening had brought Alan into contact with his breath as a means to release and retrain muscle. As his health slowly improved he also changed in his responses to the world. I noticed that he did not take control of social events in the way that he had in the past. Instead he was happy to listen and allow others to take space, often gently encouraging people who were usually quiet to emerge. His smile, rather than a flash of brilliance, became something deeper that connected with his breath and his inner being.

We had set out to heal a simple leg ulcer but in choosing to do so via breathwork, everything had changed and the whole organism had begun to heal itself of much deeper wounds.

SENSING MY OWN RESISTANCE

I began both Steve's and Alan's retraining by using techniques borrowed from the Yogis of India, as well as several of the other body-mind therapies mentioned throughout this book, including the Alexander Technique. Most of what I used, though, I had learned from a formidable old woman Swami who lived in North India. She asked me never to mention her name and out of respect for that I will refer to her simply by her title, Swamiji.

It would be unfair to retell the story of others without being prepared to disclose how I met and began to work through my own resistance. The tale of how I met Swamiji and the work we did together is essential as part of my own education about breathing.

I had already been doing Yoga for a number of years, having been taught by my teacher, Swami Venkatesananda, who had died in 1982. I thought of myself as a pretty good breather. I had decided to visit India and stay for a few months at an ashram (monastery) cradled in the foothills of the Himalayas. One day I decided to take a long walk up one of the mountains.

I was deep in reverie as I walked along a rocky ledge marvelling at the scenery all around me when suddenly something struck me dead between the shoulder blades so hard that I fell down and had my breath knocked out of me. I turned round almost in mid-fall to see a young Indian boy standing about twenty feet away with another stone in his hand. As I got my breath back I yelled at him through the pain between my shoulder blades that was searing its way through my chest. He indicated something with his head and eyes and I followed his direction. Almost hidden among the thick green jungle was what looked like another ashram. He flicked his head in the direction of this place again and then darted off.

I am not the kind of person who takes kindly to being pelted with a stone and I jumped up to run after him, which took me to the ashram he was indicating. An old woman Swami with a magnificent head of cloud white hair stood at the door. I opened my mouth to begin complaining but she broke in, surprisingly good English, 'Ah, he caught up with you – come in.' Occasionally one meets people before whom one senses resistance is futile. I think I went through some motions of explaining that I was just on a walk and wanted to get on my way and would forget about the incident with the young boy who had

by now disappeared into the dark interior of the building anyway. Despite all this I found myself sitting on a chair with the Swami's hands on my back. I always tried to be respectful so submitted and thought I would just wait until I could make my getaway.

After a while she removed her hands, made a dismissive sound, and said, 'Barely enough breathing to keep yourself alive. Come here every morning and I will teach you how to breathe.' I protested. The ashram I was staying at was a two hour walk away and besides I had already been learning breathing and there really was no need to bother her and thank you . . . and all the while I was backing away towards the front door that still stood open. In response she introduced herself and then said she would expect me by 9.30 the following morning and turned and left the room. I left too, shaking my head at the strange people one meets on one's travels in life. I had no intention of returning.

That night, back at the ashram I was staying in, I mentioned the incident to one of the old monks there. As I finished the story he stepped back wide-eyed. 'Aha, she is going to teach you. Ah, you are a lucky one, a very lucky one. This is a great blessing for you.' Fortunately he was not a man of few words and was happy to tell me everything he knew about her. Apparently she had been a famous Pranayama teacher and people had come from all over India to learn from her for many decades. Then, in the mid-fifties she had abruptly sent everyone away who came. The old monk said he himself had gone to ask for lessons but she had turned him away like all the rest. From then on, he said, he had not heard of her teaching anyone else.

Of course, with this intriguing story in mind I was at the old ashram at 9.30 a.m. sharp the next morning. I had hoped we could skip the breathing lessons and she would tell me her whole story. I am an avid story collector and I was fascinated by how a woman in India had reached such prominence in what is still largely a male domain and what had made her turn her back on it all. I tried gently to probe. But really all that happened was that she sat me in the same chair, put my body in the same position and guided the directions of my body and my attention to how and where I resisted breathing.

Despite the chunk it took out of my day I went faithfully every day from then on for the rest of my stay in India. As she turned my attention inwards I was amazed to see how much resistance my body still held, how it inhibited its own attempts to exhale completely, and I began to experience the bliss of slowly moving through the resistance to experience fuller breathing.

Only on the last few days of my stay did Swamiji begin to venture information about herself. She had entered into an arranged marriage at a very young age. Her husband had died when she was just fifteen, before any children had been born, and his family had turned her out. Returning to her own family was not an option, and hopeless and dazed she had wandered around India, finally arriving in Haridwar, one of the most sacred of Indian holy places. There she had met another wandering monk who had taken her under his wing. At first, she confided, she had thought his intentions were bad but she was hungry and exhausted. As the months wore on she came to trust him completely and he initiated her into the most ancient mysteries of Yoga. After their many years of wandering an old Englishman, one of the last of the days of the Raj I should imagine, gave them a plot of land and they built the small ashram she still lived in. Their English patron had great respect for her teacher and had also taught her English during their association.

On the night her teacher had died she had gone down to the

river to bathe and a large crow had sat on the rock above her and spoken to her. She said he was Bhasund, a sacred bird of Hindu mythology. He had taught her Pranayama (an ancient Yogic technique of controlling energy through the breath) and instructed her to teach others but only those whom he marked with his presence. She said from then on when people came to learn, Bhasund would sit on their shoulder when they first arrived and she would know by his presence that she was to teach them. If he was absent she would not teach – no matter what kind of financial inducement was offered. Then it seems, no-one who came was marked by the presence of the sacred bird. She said she had long given up hope, thinking that Bhasund's absence must mean she was to stop teaching. Then one day as she was looking out of a window, she saw me walking along the path with Bhasund sitting on my shoulder. She had quickly sent the young boy with instructions to catch up with me and bring me back to the ashram.

In my own body, as I worked with her, I encountered many of the innumerable ways in which I stood in my own way to freedom. I began to feel my own past being carried in tightened, frightened muscles and began to learn the miracle of how to encourage a muscle to release its tension. My own walk to freedom began when I met my guru in 1970. Meeting the old woman Swami, the emissary of the great bird Bhasund, hastened that journey. But it is a journey I am still walking. I did not know then that I would myself become a monk and even less that I would also be teaching breathing. One does indeed meet strange people and events on life's travels – thank God.

To begin your own journey towards the freedom of fuller breathing you can adopt some of the techniques Swamiji taught me. They are simple, effective and safe. I have adapted them slightly and included some of the directional instruc-

SENSING YOUR OWN RESISTANCE

POSE OF THE MOON

It is quite common for most therapists to ask the person to lie down on their back to begin to focus on their breathing. My own experience has been that this is not particularly useful. When we lie down the space of the thorax is reduced because the abdominal cavity spreads upward. The picture we therefore get of the breathing is one that is true only for while we are lying down and awake – too limited to be of real use. Furthermore, for most people, their lower back and pelvis areas are too stiff for this to be a comfortable posture and they actually increase tension in these areas while lying in this posture.

Adopting a Yoga posture called Pose of the Moon one can focus on how the body is moving with the breath, and even though it is not a common posture, it allows one's body to be accessible to awareness of how the body moves with the breath.

Figure 6: Pose of the Moon

Figure 7: Forward Sitting Pose

If you are unable to sit back onto your calves and heels, place a firm cushion or folded blanket under your buttocks; and if your head is unable to comfortably reach the floor, place a thickish soft covered book under your forehead. However, if you really are quite unable to get into this pose, then use its variation – sitting on a chair in a position Swamiji originally placed my own body in.

In the Forward Sitting Pose ensure that the seat of the chair is high enough to have your thighs parallel to the floor and that you have your feet flat on the floor. Then pivot forward from the hips, lean your elbows on your thighs, bend your arms at the elbows and place your hands on the opposite thighs. Be careful not to let your shoulders come up around your ears and keep your back, neck and head flowing in a straight line. Now begin to give your body direction: be careful – you are not doing something, you are simply communicating.

- *Think* of your weight releasing down.
- *Feel* your sitting bones meeting the chair and *feel* the support of the floor beneath your feet.
- *Allow* your body weight to flow down into the floor through the sitting bones and the structure of the chair and through your legs into your feet.
- *Let go* – release your hold on your spine and allow it to flow up, releasing any tension in the back of your neck, *allowing* the muscles in the back of the neck to lengthen.

Only after you feel comfortable in this posture do you drop your head forward – not pushing it, simply letting its own weight take it gently down without letting the shoulders pull up.

In any one of these postures you are ready to begin to focus on your breathing:

- Become aware of any movement you sense in your abdomen. Try not to be concerned if you feel nothing – you are not making judgements, you are becoming aware. Keep in mind all the time that you are a living being able to change.
- Then move your attention to your back, particularly the lower back. Do you sense any movement there? Can you feel any muscles in the lower back expanding and releasing with the inhalation and the exhalation? Are you aware of any movement in the spine at all?
- Is there any moment of pause between the exhalation and the next inhalation?
- Finally, begin to count your inhalation and exhalation. Are they the same length? Is one longer than the other? Make a note of all these results of your observation.

I recommend that you remain in this posture for no longer than five minutes at a time watching your breathing, then release and do something else. Come back to it later. Little and often is best in the beginning.

Here are a couple of questions students ask me at this stage which you may find helpful:

Question: After just a few seconds of watching my breath my mind wanders off and I lose focus. It's very frustrating. Is there anything I can do?

Answer: The nature of the mind is to wander – that is why we Yogis call it 'monkey-mind'. The most important thing with awareness is not to try too hard. If your mind wanders off, as soon as you become aware that it has wandered you gently bring it back to focusing on breathing. The trick in not getting frustrated is to realise that this is the way the mind now functions, accept that. Gradually, as you work with awareness over months and years the mind will become retrained. The only thing that is making you frustrated is that you want it NOW. Awareness, I'm afraid, is not a quick fix. It is a process that will change everything but we have to submit to the process, surrender to ourselves, accept ourselves.

Question: Very soon after focusing on my breathing I start getting real feelings of panic. To be honest, these often make me just break off and do something else. Is there any way of approaching this problem?

Answer: You are fortunate – it usually takes people months to become aware that they are in a chronic state of panic! Panic, discomfort, pain – these are things we use as catalysts for movement and change. If you're sitting on a lawn on a nice warm summer day, drifting off, muscles relaxed – there is no need to move at all. Then an ant climbs up your skirt and bites you on that soft tender part of your thigh. No matter how relaxed you were you jump up instantly, propelled by the pain and discomfort, and there is a sense of urgency and panic to the situation. All these were there to get you to move. What you do when you feel the panic is to move in the direction you have always moved – anywhere as long as it is away from the pain. Then you do something else, distracting yourself by getting involved in another task, preferably a trivial one. I know sometimes when I encounter my own resistance I suddenly and urgently believe that the kitchen floor needs mopping or that my desk drawer has to be tidied as a matter of great importance.

Now I am asking you *not* to give in to that impulse to immediately move away – to stay with the pain long enough to find the right direction to move in. Moving away from the pain by distracting oneself means the pain will always be mysterious to us, an unknown quantity in our lives that has the power to strike at any time. We have to turn and face it and know it. The pain, you see, will point us in the right direction if we connect well enough with it. So, stay with the panic but instead of getting involved with it see if you can observe it in the same way that you observe your breathing: simply watching, locating it physically. Then, take your breath into it, breathe into it, try and breathe right through it, exhale it. In this way rather than looking away you are allowing the panic to have its full life and communicate its message to you.

A DIFFERENT RESULT

Our breathing will change as we begin to do something different from that which we are doing to breathe now. Once we have turned in the direction of freedom, freedom of the breath, freedom from tension, freedom from holding onto our past, we are on a new road. We have to become remarkably aware because for each of us there will be twists and turns in the road that are different from everybody else's.

A great educationalist, John Dewey, wrote about this:

> Hence the work of intelligence in observing consequences and in
> revising and readjusting habits, even the best of good habits, can
> never be foregone . . . The assumption of a stably uniform envi-
> ronment (even the hankering for one) expresses a fiction due to
> attachment to old habits.

Because when we change our breathing we change everything,
it is not a process with an end, it can 'never be foregone'. We
begin this walk to freedom with no end to the road in sight, and
Dewey had something wonderful to say about that too:

> To reach an end we must take our mind off it and attend to the act
> which is next to be performed. We must make that the end.

BREATH AND THE MIND

Modern psychiatry and psychotherapy will continue to flounder in misplaced practice and irrelevant theories until they recognise the simple truth that the core of man's psyche is located not in his head, but in his total organism.

MALCOLM BROWN PhD

The Dark Age of Europe, which began with the fall of Rome in AD 476, saw the devastating bubonic plague sweep through country after country, killing almost all of its victims. People emptied the cities and retreated to the countryside to try and escape. As plague after plague followed, Europe became a bleak landscape. Only after the year 1000 AD. – and the emergence of the Middle Ages – did some fresh creativity begin to emerge in literature and thought, and by the 1500s there was a resurgence of scientific progress that was to revitalize European culture. In 1596 a man was to step onto this stage who would fundamentally alter our view of ourselves, his name was René Descartes.

Plato, the ancient Greek philosopher and another great thinker who influenced European philosophy, believed in the duality of mind and matter, and that truth resided in the world of Knowledge. However it was Descartes, often viewed as the father of modern philosophy, who gave European culture a basis of separation of mind and body that most people of the Western world labour under still. Descartes believed in the existence of mind 'stuff' and body 'stuff'. But the fact that the mind, the reasoning capacity of the human being, was able to follow certain rules, to deliberate before taking action, to defer gratification, all suggested to him that there was something unique about the mind that distinguished it from the body. To Descartes the body was like a machine and the mind was its soul, localized in the brain. As he remarked:

> . . . It is however easily proved that the soul feels those things that affect the body not insofar as it is in each member of the body, but only insofar as it is in the brain, where the nerves by their movements convey to it diverse actions of the external objects which touch part of the body.

This notion of separation between body and mind was so firmly held by Steve and Alan that they grappled to come to terms with the fact that what had happened to them emotionally had led to a reaction in their bodies and vice versa. Steve believed that his panic attacks were 'all in the mind' and had difficulty grasping that every cell and molecule of his being held his mind and had organized itself around his experiences. Alan at first thought that what I was saying was that his leg ulcer was 'all in the mind'. What I was saying in reality was that the mind was in his leg ulcer as much as it was in any other part of his body, including his frozen breathing.

With both of them, understanding the flow of human history and how we got to this now disputed body-mind separation was a great help in understanding how their breathing was a state of both body and mind.

Descartes laid the groundwork, and in the late seventeenth century a scientific genius, Isaac Newton, published his masterpiece, the *Principia* which took us on the final step of commitment to body-mind separation. During that era, the most sophisticated mechanism available was the clock, which epitomises precision and order. The view that Newton presented through his *Principia* was of a universe obeying material laws with clockwork precision. This became known as the Newtonian view. This view did not, of course, remain confined to the scientific community – the West as a whole embraced it and even now finds it hard to let go. We still use everyday expressions like 'mind over matter' without pausing to wonder whether mind *is* perhaps matter.

To Newton matter – that which you and I and this whole vast universe are made up of – consisted of 'solid, impenetrable, movable particles', to use his own words. The Newtonian 'laws' gave us a new framework in which science could study a whole range of things – including living organisms like us. It was within this framework that an extraordinary amount of knowledge about our world was gathered. Using its principles gave us the means for all kinds of discoveries – from inventing the steam engine to cracking the 'genetic code' with the discovery of DNA.

Unfortunately this framework also gave rise to a totally mechanistic and materialistic view of the body which was seen as nothing more than a collection of particles (albeit a complicated one), pushing and pulling each other. And this pushing and pulling, scientists told us, could be measured and determined just as the movement of the planets around the sun could be measured and determined. Newton had discovered a clear connection between cause and effect – all matter moved in accord with strict mathematical laws. All mystery was gone and the idea of the world as an organic living entity became confined to mysticism and religion. Gradually, in our minds and in the 'mind' of medicine, we humans also became the parts within parts of the machine: cogs in a wheel that rumbled on regardless of what we thought or felt. This material world became the only world, the only 'real' world worth investigating, and that investigation was narrowly confined to that which could be properly measured. Things like compassion and tenderness or anxiety and frustration have no measurement scale, so science at best ignored them and at worst denied their impact on the 'real' world.

Fortunately for us though, Nature has a way of making apparent what is real and a few chinks began to appear in the Newtonian framework. In the nineteenth century two scientists discovered and investigated electric and magnetic phenomena. This gave rise to identifying a new type of force, electromagnetism, that just would not fit into the mechanistic model of Newton. Creeping into science came the awkward notion that nothing was static, everything was subject to change – the outcome of which was not always possible to determine or measure. What appeared to be inert matter within the Newtonian framework was suddenly springing to life.

Experiments took place within this Newtonian framework but the results catapulted themselves out of it. Late last century a scientist experimented on sea urchins with some disturbing results. In the Newtonian model any structure can only develop from what is present in the egg it began in. But when a scientist killed one cell of the two-celled embryo of a sea urchin, the structure which grew was not a half or parts of a sea-urchin as would be expected: instead it was a whole, if somewhat smaller, sea-urchin! Somehow this embryo had managed to regenerate and re-organize itself, even though no mechanism could then or now be found to determine such self-organization and regeneration of damaged tissue. The sea-urchin had found a way of being a whole sea urchin whatever limitations science wanted to impose.

Many such experiments took place despite which science remained machine-minded until the 1930s when another genius came along, one who was to write:

> . . . Newton, forgive me; you found the only way which, in your age, was possible for a man of the highest thought and creative power. The concepts, which you created, are even today still guiding our thinking although we know they will have to be replaced by others farther removed from the sphere of immediate experience, if we are to aim at a profounder understanding . . .

This genius was Albert Einstein. In this century he challenged the old mechanistic model with his theory of general relativity. The clockwork universe became subject to shifting and warping. Time and space ceased to be fixed, determined entities. The 'real' world began to look not so real after all. Life became more of a changing, dynamic, living force rather than a machine that appeared out of nowhere fully constructed. Alongside Einstein's theory of relativity another body of science was gaining momentum: quantum physics. Quantum physics, which revolutionized our view of matter, of the hard, real universe, is the science of studying very small particles, particles smaller than atoms which are called quantum particles.

Scaled down by quantum theory, Newton's hard atoms became waves and particles. Suddenly the materialistic view of the universe disappeared – astonishingly revealing that matter has less substance than Newton had supposed. Indeed, as scientists investigate the quantum field theory even the waves and particles are dissolving and being replaced by vibrations of

an invisible field of energy. One of these great new physicists explained it succinctly:

> By getting to smaller and smaller units, we do not come to funda-
> mental units, or indivisible units, but we <u>do</u> come to a point
> where the division has no meaning.
>
> WERNER HEISENBERG

THE BODY AS THE BEARER OF THOUGHT

Even though this new physics has been with us for seventy years it is still hard for us now as we approach the turn of the century, to really accept that the body and the mind are one organism rather than two separate units that sometimes communicate with each other.

Alan did not become convinced until he experienced the tension in his body as a legacy of his own history. Using awareness techniques borrowed from Yoga and some of the other body-work systems I mentioned in the previous chapter, Alan and I began to work on his breathing. This allowed him, for the first time in his life, to observe his own body.

What emerged during the treatments that followed was that Alan had a violent father who had frequently been physically abusive to his mother. His older brother had responded to this tension by becoming like his father and had bullied Alan as a child. Added to this was the fact that his brother had excelled at sports – which their father admired – while Alan was happier with maths and science. Gradually he had closed himself off and withdrawn inward, swallowed the pain and become convinced that he was not worthy of the nourishment of breath. Alan had organized his breathing around his father's lack of love and approval. The process of becoming conscious of that had required Alan to first become conscious of how he was constricting his breathing – and in so doing narrowing his potential.

One day when Alan came for a session he was very animated. He had understood what I was talking about from an intellectual point of view, but he had to have a very direct experience of it to make it his own. The evening before his treatment he had gone to visit a couple who were friends of his. During the meal they had started to argue with one another – nothing too serious but a genuine disagreement nonetheless. Alan said he caught his body tightening up and at first he also caught himself trying to stop the argument by injecting a note of jollity, as a means of drawing their attention away from their disagreement. Then he had stopped and simply sat back, allowing them to continue their wrangle, while he watched his breathing. Very quickly, he said, it changed and became more shallow as his stomach and jaw tensed as if in anticipation of something terrible to come.

This was an ideal situation for Alan to observe himself in. Domestic tension had been the start of his own tension-building process, and even though this was not his parents he was observing so there was no real threat, his body was responding in its habitual way to the situation. He began, if not by having an experience of wholeness, at least to experience the whole of his body as the bearer of his thoughts and emotions.

In the field of breathing a great deal of research supports the non-dual position. In *Behavioral and Psychological Approaches to Breathing Disorders* edited by Timmons and Ley, in a chapter entitled Breathing and Feeling the author Dr Ashley Conway of the Department of Psychiatry at Charing Cross Hospital, gives the following quote from a study:

> . . . if individuals are unable to disclose traumas . . . they must constantly hold back or inhibit their thoughts, feelings, and

behaviours from others and, on occasion, themselves. Not discussing the traumatic event with others then, represents a significant long-term physical stressor.

PENNEBAKER AND SUSMAN

What the above researchers appear to be saying is that not discussing a traumatic event with a friend or another intimate, creates a 'significant' physical stress. In my language as a Yogi, I would say the trauma is being expressed in and communicated by the body very eloquently through tense muscles and inappropriate breathing habits.

Outside stressors are constant for all of us, but our way of dealing with them can change dramatically – and breath is one of the most powerful means of both investigating the trauma and making the change. Before we look at a common breathing disorder and how it may be a manifestation of body/mind oneness, try an awareness exercise to see if you can experience this oneness through your breath.

BODY-MIND AWARENESS EXERCISE

- Adopt the Forward Sitting Pose given in the previous chapter, following the body directions until your mind is able to focus on the breathing.
- Become aware of how much your abdomen and/or chest expands with each breath, as well as the frequency of inhalations and exhalations. Try not to count them at this stage – simply allow your mind to become familiar with them, so that they are easily recognizable to you.
- Now, for just a few seconds think of something that frightens you – either something from your past or a fear you have now. Conjure up as vivid an image as possible of your fear, and as soon as you have it switch your attention

back to your breathing. (As I am unable to swim or go under water without holding my nose, I am frightened of physically entering large bodies of water. So, whenever I have to do this exercise I think of being in the sea or in a large lake in which the water is not calm.)

- Did you notice any change at all? Did simply holding an image of something frightening change the rate or depth (or both) of your breathing?

I have never had a student who has not responded to the above exercise by immediately modifying their breathing. You can use it equally well by trying just the opposite:

- Remain in Sitting Forward Pose observing your breath.
- This time conjure up an image of something you find pleasant, loving or relaxing. Hold the image in your mind for a few seconds and again switch your awareness to your breathing and ask the same questions of yourself and note the answers.

BREATHING AND THE BODY-MIND

I would not suggest that asthma or any other disorder is merely 'psychological' or a case of 'mind over matter'. That kind of Cartesian separation of mind and body has been displaced. The mind does not 'act' on the body – I believe, as all Yogis do, and as modern physicists like Heisenberg do, that *the division has no meaning.* There is a whole organism at work. When I conjure up an image of something wonderful (or something frightening) division disappears and the whole organism holds that vision: the mind as a picture or image, the body as relaxed (or tense) muscle and deeper (or more shallow) breathing.

Alan's past was not simply held in memory cells situated somewhere in his brain and 'acting' on his body. His whole body participated in holding that past. The impoverished circulation which had led to poor wound healing and his restrained breathing were his body both holding and communicating that past. His disconnected relationships in which he never disclosed himself verbally but infused every social occasion with enough jollity to avoid verbalizing his underlying tension were also the holding of that pain. As the body released the mind released and the social persona released. One was not influencing or acting on the other – *the division had no meaning*

With this in mind we can examine body–mind disorders like asthma to reveal the whole organism's response and its relationship to breathing.

ASTHMA

Asthma is a common breathing disorder. Indeed, about five per cent of the population has asthma and that figure is on the increase. It is a frightening disorder characterized by periodic 'attacks' during which breathing becomes severely impeded. During an asthma attack the cells lining the airways become inflamed causing constriction and the accumulation of mucus – narrowing the passage for the air to pass through on its journey to the lungs. Commonly asthma begins in childhood and it accounts for more lost schooldays than any other childhood illness. However it is on the increase in adults and the mortality rate is rising, particularly among older patients.

An attack of asthma can have any number of 'triggers' like over-exertion, weather changes, allergies to certain pollens, animals or foods, household dust and moulds, a smoky atmosphere etc. Finding the trigger(s) is important so that severe attacks can be avoided.

One of my patients developed mild adult onset asthma and his GP had prescribed the usual bronchodilators for him to take in order to inhibit the severity of an attack. He had reported that the attacks always began in the morning shortly after he got up, while he was still at home exposed to the same things he had been exposed to all night although he never woke up wheezing. We did the usual breathing awareness techniques and then he telephoned me very triumphantly announcing he had discovered the 'cause' of his asthma. He noticed that while shaving as usual with his electric razor, he had started wheezing and coughing and was unable to sustain the extended exhalation I had taught him. This made him stop and examine what he was doing *at the time* of the attack. It was then that he realized his razor made an extremely fine dust out of his morning shadow which he constantly tapped or blew, and that it was this fine dust that induced the wheezing! I congratulated him on his detective work but suggested that many men use electric razors without developing asthma and that while it might be a trigger it was probably not a 'cause'.

No-one actually knows what the cause of asthma is, despite enormous research. Initially it was thought to be a bronchial spasm that could be triggered by any one of the factors mentioned above. Deeper probing has revealed that inflammation of the airways is present *before* the trigger is present and that this inflammation is an immune response. The theory put forward below by Dr Buteyko, that this immune response is the body defending itself in the face of falling carbon dioxide levels, has not yet been widely accepted by the medical establishment. Modern medicine functions by always searching out 'the single cause': the virus, the bacteria, the gene, etc., that can be defined as the single cause of the disease. It is science based on the old Newtonian idea of a cause – effect relationship being absolute. Yet 'the single cause' of most cancers and chronic and

fatal diseases like Multiple Sclerosis still eludes the researchers. I often wonder if the causes of these illnesses are as multitudinous as we are and the cause is different in each of us?

Working on a different hypothesis, one in which cause and symptom are two ends of the same stick, the 'single cause' becomes less relevant than inhibiting the symptoms.

THE BUTEYKO METHOD

One of the most controversial treatments for asthma to have emerged in recent years is the Buteyko method. To Professor Buteyko, cause and symptom are intimately linked and his method treats both. Originally the method was devised to treat high blood pressure and during its use it was discovered it also treated asthma. The medical profession is still debating the Buteyko method and largely refusing to accept it. Millions of asthma sufferers all over the world, however, attest to its efficacy and a trial of the method done in Brisbane, Australia, by the Australian Foundations of Asthma Association, showed an astonishing 90 per cent decrease in the use of relief drugs needed to deal with the symptoms. The Buteyko group also showed a 71 per cent improvement of their symptoms as opposed to a 14 per cent improvement in the placebo group. Buteyko's method involves the sufferer in changing their breathing habits rather than relying on medication to overcome their symptoms. This is because Buteyko claims it is *the way* we breathe that is causing the inflammation, restriction and mucus build-up in the air passages.

To understand the Buteyko method you have to recall the information about the oxygen/carbon dioxide balance. Unfortunately carbon dioxide has been dismissed as a waste gas that we simply breathe out. Not true. Carbon dioxide is the 'driver' of our respiratory system. The body is not monitoring the levels of oxygen as meticulously as it does the levels of carbon dioxide. Carbon dioxide levels, and not oxygen levels, will determine our rate of breathing. This is not only because we use carbon dioxide in our acid – alkaline pH balancing mechanism but because it is carbon dioxide that helps 'unbind' oxygen in the blood and deliver it to the tissues in the process of internal respiration.

According to Buteyko asthma is caused by hyperventilation which has upset the delicate balance between oxygen and carbon dioxide to the extent that the delivery of oxygen from the blood to the cells is slowed down. What then happens is a vicious cycle: the brain and internal organs are deprived of the oxygen they need which causes the body to breathe more which lowers further the level of carbon dioxide. The body then tries to protect itself from these falling levels of carbon dioxide by restricting the air passages. In Alexander Stalmatski's book, *Freedom from Asthma* he says,

> Asthma is the message your body is sending you to stop over-breathing. It makes you wheeze, constricts your bronchotubes, makes extra mucus, decreases your lung capacity – all in an attempt to stop you breathing out so much carbon dioxide.

The first defence, Buteyko says, will make you feel tight, wheezy and/or breathless and the second defence will make you start coughing. As you struggle to breath in more air the constriction will become worse. The solution for Buteyko is to have the asthma patient slow down their breathing and allow for the natural pause in breathing between exhalation and inhalation, thus giving the body an opportunity to normalize its carbon dioxide level. His method then goes one step further to retrain the brain to adjust to the new carbon dioxide levels.

We know from other research that if overbreathing (even mild hyperventilation) continues for a few hours or days, the

control centre in the brain re-sets itself to maintain lower levels of carbon dioxide. This means that the body has lost a fine tuning mechanism and fails to adjust accurately for changes in activity. The Buteyko method takes this into account and works to gently re-condition the control mechanism to get used to the higher, but normal, levels of carbon dioxide.

Something similar was happening to Steve. While on the football field his need for oxygen was increased so the body responded by increasing his breathing. Because he was then involved in physical activity, the rate at which the body converted the oxygen to carbon dioxide was also increased.

Then Steve would stop playing and carry on with other activities. The panic attacks would happen most often while he was relaxing or just as he was going to sleep. Steve's breathing habits (longer inhalations, mouth breathing, etc.) meant that his body was taking in oxygen in excess of what could be converted to carbon dioxide. The low carbon dioxide levels in the blood caused the cerebral blood vessels to constrict, reducing the flow of blood – and oxygen – to the brain. This would produce an increase in breathing as the body tried to balance these levels and Steve would experience this increase as a panic attack. The constriction of the blood vessels to the brain is also why many hyperventilators experience feelings of depersonalisation around (either before or after or both) an extreme attack of hyperventilation.

ASTHMA, HYPERVENTILATION AND THE BODY-MIND CONNECTION

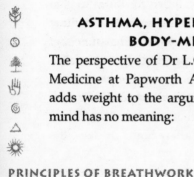

The perspective of Dr L.C. Lum of the Department of Chest Medicine at Papworth Addenbrookes Hospital, Cambridge, adds weight to the argument that the division of body and mind has no meaning:

A careful history usually suggests that the habit of overbreathing is established early in childhood. Eighty per cent of the author's female patients give a history of defective bonding with one or both parents – more often the father. The parent may be unable to show physical affection, be overly strict, alcoholic, a wife beater, or just too busy to bond with the child. The child tries to attract attention, or avoid censure, by becoming perfectionist or over meticulous. In the remaining 20 per cent, a history of breathing troubles (asthma, bronchitis, emphysema) or life-threatening illness is often found in the patient's family. Similarly, there may be a loss of a parent by death or divorce. Insecurity tends to carry over into adult relationships. Women, no matter how successful or attractive, almost always have a basic insecurity. The habit is often passed from mother to daughter. Hyperventilating girls tend to be brought up by hyperventilating mothers. Men differ. They are often achievers who set goals above their abilities or fail to adjust to changing work patterns, a state pithily described as promotion depression.[1]

While I feel Dr Lum's gender division is a decade or two out of date, I certainly appreciate this observation from so eminent a medical practitioner on the relationship between an individual's personal history and between mind, body and breath.

PRESSURE AND THE BODY

If Buteyko is right, if asthma is a defence mechanism of the body in response to hyperventilation (breathing in excess of the body's needs), then asthma as a body-mind response cannot be ruled out. What the body is communicating through asthma in some people, was being expressed by Steve's body as panic attacks. Both are an indication of heightened oxygen levels and lowered carbon dioxide levels which cause fine balancing mechanisms to go awry.

Any doctor would agree that *hyperventilation is a perfectly normal response to stress*. If you tried the test earlier in the chapter you would have noticed that when you thought of something frightening your breathing became more rapid and shallow – if it had been a real situation you would have gone onto hyperventilation that would have lasted as long as the stressor was present. We know that often hyperventilation persists after the stressor is removed: when its balancing mechanisms are challenged far enough, the body begins to throw up signals like asthma and panic attacks. Supressing the signals with medication is of course necessary so that the signal does not kill the messenger. But addressing the problem completely should not stop there.

The Buteyko method seems to be having excellent results in reducing the symptoms of asthma for many sufferers. Add to this other bodywork techniques like Yoga, the Alexander Technique, Bioenergetics or any other of the numerous mind-body techniques now available for addressing the body's organization around its history, and you begin to effect a release of the tension that the body-mind organism is holding. This creates a more fundamental healing process because you are addressing the habits of tension in the whole organism.

I often ask new classes of Yoga students to count their inhalations and exhalations. In the twenty years that I have been teaching Yoga, the overwhelming majority of students have said that their inhalation lasts longer than their exhalation, and that they are not experiencing a pause between the exhalation and the next inhalation. Not all of them are suffering from asthma (although it is a common reason for many people taking up Yoga) but most of them will cite stress, fatigue and aches and pains as their reasons for joining a Yoga class. The body's way of communicating its distress varies – asthma and chronic fatigue may be the extremes of that communication.

Chronic, hidden tension is a body-mind phenomenon and it appears that there is a whole organism response that in one person may be asthma, in another fatigue, and in another muscle cramps or panic attacks. The entire organism acts as one – both to adjust to the change and to communicate its distress. Any division we may perceive between body and mind really does have no meaning.

Conscious breathing offers the most direct route to the unconscious tensions that we all hold. It also offers a means of release from those tensions that involves the entire body-mind organism, inviting it to experience its wholeness.

1. L.C. Lum. Hyperventilation Syndromes, *Behavioral and Psychological Approaches to Breathing Disorders.*

BREATHING
TOWARDS CLARITY

It could be best felt when it could not clearly be seen.

THOMAS HARDY

Full respiration is based on contact with others
as well as with one's self.

STANLEY KELEMAN

What we can see is that our breathing is not separate from our collective human history and evolution, our individual past or our environment. We cannot escape any of these, nor should we want to – for it is the combination of these factors that makes each of us mysteriously unique while we remain so alike. What we can do is begin to intervene in our chronic stress-holding patterns in order to liberate our breathing – because breathing is not a matter of the lungs moving, but the whole body moving: contracting and expanding and resting in equilibrium.

When I began my own personal journey towards fuller breathing, one of the hardest things to do was to confront old holding patterns in my body. Each of those holding patterns seemed to be not only holding onto my past but also often protecting me from it. My memories had become the tension in my muscles and connective tissues of my body. Ron Kurtz, founder of Hakomi – a body-centred psychotherapy – gives this sage advice:

The first step towards changing oneself is a step backwards.

This step backwards is not easy but it is infinitely rewarding. Only once we have gone back, into ourselves, can we begin to move forward, to breathe more freely and open ourselves to the vitality and life that comes with each breath.

In this chapter we will look at different segments of the body, how we commonly hold tension in these areas and how we can gently begin to release them on our own. Then we will look at experiencing full body breathing and the whole body experience.

To begin with, however, let us look at two body types which are extremes that inhibit full body breathing. These are the 'rigid' and 'collapsed' bodies described by Stanley Keleman, in his book *Emotional Anatomy*.

The rigid body, Keleman says, is the body braced against disapproval and insult. The collapsed body is the body that has caved in under the weight of such disapproval and insult, dragging the diaphragm muscle downward. The first posture is the one which is commonly approved of at school as 'standing up straight' and the second is what we do we when we have failed (or rebelled against) 'standing up straight'. In fact neither of these represent the body standing up straight. As Ron Colyer, an Alexander teacher writes:

It is usually assumed that this kind of stiff standing enables us to 'stand up straight'. Objective observation shows standing is neither straight nor up in this condition . . . This stiffening way of standing has a deleterious effect on the breathing – which is counter to what the practitioner is seeking. This kind of posture also resembles in many ways the startle reflex which is one of our most primitive responses to fear. It is interesting that this method of standing finds such favour with military authorities. People may be more easily subjugated and their individuality more effectively suppressed if they can be induced to assume the physiological attitude which most closely corresponds to the fear state.[1]

Begin by getting an idea of your own general posture. Next time you have stripped off your clothing take a few moments to look at yourself in a full-length mirror. Examine both the full frontal and side views. You will probably find that you are not at either of these extremes of rigid or collapsed but somewhere in the middle with elements of each: your shoulders may be raised and/or rotated slightly forward; or your neck may incline forward and your chin jut out; your lumbar spine might sweep inward and your lower back lift up; etc. Try not to become involved in making judgements, simply observe for observation's sake. Observe your shoulders for a moment, see if they lift and descend – or move at all – with your breathing.

Once you have a visual image of your holding patterns it is time to go for a deeper experience: looking inward at yourself. One of the ancient texts of Hinduism called the *Brihadaranyaka Upanishad* says that one of the last responsibilities of the soul just before the body is born is to '*break open the senses from the inside out*'. Turning these senses back in on ourselves is our very first step towards self-knowledge. It is also the most powerful means available for bringing about change. One of the great codifiers of the philosophy and practice of Yoga was a sage named Patanjali, who said that *awareness changes everything*. This is borne out in modern quantum physics which verifies that matter behaves differently in the presence of an observer.

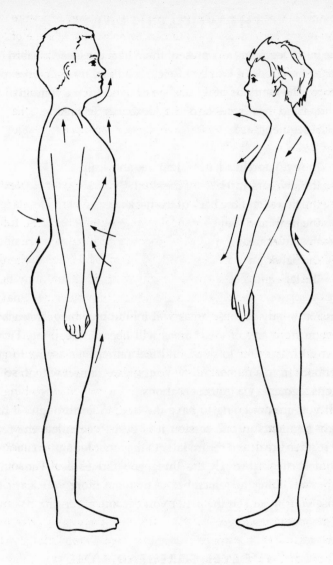

Figure 8: Posture

THE WHOLE IN PARTS

The body segments as I present them here are loosely based on the observations of Wilhelm Reich, modified by my own experience. The methods of release are derived from a combination of Yoga and the directions of the Alexander Technique.

The segments are:

- the eyes, forehead, nose, temples and scalp
- the jaw, ears and base of the skull
- the throat and the back of the neck
- the heart and lungs
- the navel area
- the pelvic area
- the legs and feet

Tension in any of these areas will inhibit breathing. Releasing tension from any of these areas will liberate breathing. From now on it is better to sense and feel rather than trying to get feedback from a mirror. Allow yourself to connect with the different segments via inner sensations.

If you are not going to have the time to go through all the body segments in one session it is best to complete the first three, then break and return later to the other four after running a quick check through the three you did earlier. The most important thing to remember is that the more you learn to sense your inner self the better you become at sensing it – and the deeper you will go.

THE EYES, FOREHEAD, NOSE, TEMPLES AND SCALP

Begin investigating and releasing these segments seated on a dining room type chair, with a pillow tucked in the small of

your back to give you comfortable support. To sense and feel
tension in this segment check through the following:

- If you were to locate the 'I' of 'I am' would you locate it in
  this head/brain centre? Many people forget that the 'I' is a
  whole body 'I' – not simply a brain 'I'. Ask yourself,
  'When I use the word 'I' where do I locate it?'
- Do the outer corners of the eyes feel pinned back towards
  the temples and do the lower lids of the eyes feel as if they
  are working, holding up the eye, focusing?
- Now check your breathing, what is its rate, where are you
  breathing, where are you experiencing movement?
- Go back to the eyes and feel their relationship with the
  forehead and the relationship of the forehead with the
  scalp. Where you sense tightness can you consciously let it
  go as you let the breath go during an inhalation? Can you
  feel the sensation of a slow release?
- If you wear spectacles all the time it is important to leave
  them on and sense whether this segment experiences any
  tension in 'holding' them.

Now you are ready to do a simple exercise with the eyes. The
important thing is to do this very slowly and with great attention to your inner self. Remaining seated try the following:

- Let your eyes rest on the floor about six feet in front of
  you. Try not look *at* the floor but rather look *through* it.
  This is called Tratak in Yoga – The Restful Gaze. There
  should be no effort here, you are looking 'through' the
  floor with a restful gaze. Gradually become aware of
  everything you see in the periphery of your vision.
  Without moving your gaze from its spot on the floor,
  become aware of your whole field of vision. As you do

78

that you will almost immediately become aware of a subtle desire to allow your eyes to flicker around. Resist the impulse but do not suppress it – be aware of it, give it full and complete acknowledgement, but simply remain gazing at the floor in front of you.

- Now gently turn your head around to the right, not too far. Again the important thing in this exercise is that you do not let your eyes dart forward or backward. That impulse for the eyes to dart around is one of our old fear impulses at work – trying always to check forward and backward for any signs of danger. Be aware that you are in no danger now and you are allowing your restful gaze to flow with the movement of your head. Repeat the same thing to the left side and then bring your gaze back to the centre.
- Check in with your breathing, has it changed as you are doing this?

Try and repeat parts of this exercise through the day. Stop wherever you are and let your gaze just rest some distance away – looking through rather than at. Watch the impulse to let your eyes dart forward and backward and resist it while you continue with Tratak, The Restful Gaze. Check in with your breathing.

Maintaining the restful gaze, turn your awareness to your nose:

- Feel the cool air entering through both nostrils as you breathe in, feel it hitting the back of your throat before it descends and warms. Then feel the warm air that rises up from the throat leaving through both your nostrils.
- Do both nostrils carry the same amount of air, or is one feeling slightly closed? Which one? This is a perfectly normal phenomenon. One nostril is always slightly more

PRINCIPLES OF BREATHWORK

dilated than the other and this switches throughout the day. The way the body accomplishes this switch is by flooding the capillaries in one nostril with slightly more blood than the other, causing them to swell and thereby reduce the size of the nostril.

- If you are unsure, just lightly clip shut one nostril and feel the flow of breath in the other, then repeat on the other side. Another effective way of measuring is just to breathe out onto a small hand-held mirror and you will see there is a greater area of vapour left on the mirror on one side – the side that is more open at the time of the test.

One of the most common reasons for breathing disorders and mouth breathing is one or both of the nostrils being constantly blocked. There could be a number of reasons for this: a cold during which you are producing mucus; an allergy response which is causing the same thing; nasal polyps; or a deviated septum.

Nasal polyps: A persistent swelling in the lining of the nose due to lingering sinus congestion. If you suspect this it is advisable to visit a good herbalist to see if they can help clear the infection and establish its source, or see an ear, nose and throat specialist. It is extremely difficult to establish regular, free breathing when this front line of defence, the nose, is obstructed.

Deviated septum: The septum is the wall in the nose between the nostrils and it normally runs in a straight line from the nostrils to the base of the skull at the back. However, it is not uncommon for the septum to deviate from this straight line and obstruct the breathing. This could happen as a result of an accident or it could be congenital.

Steve had broken his nose during a game many years before coming to see me which had caused a deviated septum and blocked his breathing in one nostril. Although Steve had no

clear memory of it, I suspect that he became a mouth breather after his accident. During our treatment he consulted an ear, nose and throat specialist who successfully surgically corrected the deviation.

In winter, when many people in the Northern hemisphere use central heating the atmosphere in most homes can become far too dry to keep the lining of the nostrils comfortably moist. It is advisable to constantly check your nose, whether at home or at work, to ensure that it is moist and happy. If it begins to feel dry and tender introduce a humidifier to add some moisture to the atmosphere.

THE JAW, EARS AND BASE OF THE SKULL

This can be an area of old and chronic tensions. The incredibly powerful muscles of the jaw may have become accustomed to clenching the teeth, and the tongue may have become accustomed to a remarkable rigidity. I sat through a meeting with seven men once during which five of them articulated everything they had to say through clenched teeth – and this was not a stressful occasion. Tension in this area is not surprising when you consider the number of times people suppress what they want to say for what it is acceptable to say, or how often we suppress expressions of love, tenderness or pain.

Remaining seated on the chair now turn your attention to the jaw, ears and the base of the skull at the back of your head:

- Begin by taking your attention to the base of the skull. You will probably find that this area feels as if it is being pulled down by the back of the neck, giving your chin a forward and upward tilt and pulling down on the back of your head. Once you have become aware of these sensations of the back of the head being pulled down, check in with your breathing, feeling its rhythm and rate.

- Now, allow the base of the skull to become 'unhinged' and float upwards. As you do that the chin might drop slightly and your forehead and top of your head tilt forward.
- As this release happens check in the with your breathing again.
- Next we come to the jaw. Are your teeth meeting? Even if they are meeting just lightly it indicates the presence of tension in the powerful muscles of the jaw.
- Check your tongue – is it pressing against the roof of your mouth or is it lying relaxed and making more contact with the floor of the mouth?
- To release the jaw you can try a variation of a Yoga posture called The Lion's Breath. Breathe in through your nose, and as you breathe out open your mouth wide and throw your tongue out as far as you can. If you do it a few times you should begin to make a sound with it – like the roar of a lion coming from deep down within you.
- If the Lion's Breath feels too extreme, try this instead. Hold out your right hand and keeping the fingers together bring the thumb away from the fingers. Lift the hand so the palm is turned towards your face and place the thumb alongside the jawbone on the right and the fingers alongside the jawbone on your left, then rest the whole inner edge of the hand resting on your chin.
- Now gently exert a downward pressure with your hand letting your jaw loosen and your hand pull it down. Synchronize this movement with your breath, breathing out as you pull the jaw down.
- Once you have repeated this exercise a few times check that the base of the skull has not latched itself to that downward pull again – if it has let it release. Check in with your breathing and take your attention to your cheeks and ears.

- Become aware of how 'set' the muscles of the cheeks may be. Often these muscles hold an anticipatory tension for speech or smiling. Simply become aware of the tension and as you look at it feel it melting away.
- Become aware of your ears. Now employ your powerful imagination and imagine that you are breathing not through the nose, but through the ears. Feel that each inhalation and exhalation is happening through the ears and that you are breathing a sense of peace into the ears and allowing it to fill the skull and mouth and flow down through the throat.

THE THROAT AND BACK OF THE NECK

The throat and neck represent the slender link between the head and the heart. Again this is a depository of much tension. Begin by just becoming aware of the whole throat and neck and how the head balances on top of the neck. Then gently proceed with checking and releasing this area:

- Become aware of any feelings of constriction in the throat. Remaining aware of this feeling breathe in through the nose, feeling the cool air flowing down your throat. As you breathe out, allow your jaw to drop comfortably and release the breath with a long whispered 'Ahhhh . . .' As the whispered 'ahhhh' flows out feel the tension in the throat releasing and leaving with the outbreath. Let the 'ahhhh' sound last as long as the outbreath lasts, allowing yourself to breathe out completely. With each 'ahhhh' sound feel that your throat is opening more and more.
- Become aware of the back of the neck. The back of the neck and the lumbar region of the spine are the most mobile areas of the back and problems in one usually reflect problems in the other. Begin by feeling your sitting bones

and feet contacting the support beneath them. Breathe in, and as you breathe out release your weight down through your sitting bones into the chair and down through your legs into the floor. Repeat this focus for two or three breaths and then as your weight has released allow the muscles of the neck to release and lengthen.

- To continue the release of tension in the muscles at the back of the neck breathe in and as you breathe out allow your head to drop forward. Be careful not to push it down – simply let its own weight carry it down. Keep releasing it for a full inhalation and exhalation and then slowly raise your head and allow it to balance on top of the neck rather than fall down into it at the back.

- Next, breathe in and as you breathe out allow your head to release to the right, dropping your right ear towards your

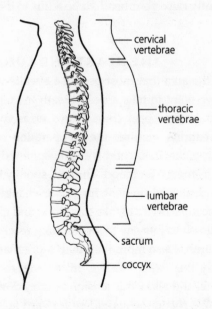

Figure 9: The Spine

right shoulder. Again, you are not pushing down – there is no goal to accomplish other than release – so simply let the head go. You will feel a gentle stretch up the left side of the neck. Be sure to allow your shoulders to release. Again hold this for a full inhalation and exhalation and slowly raise the head. Repeat this to the other side.

- Muscles that can become quite tight – particularly if you are an upper chest breather (like many asthmatics) are muscles of the neck. To help these release you can turn your head as if you are going to look over your right shoulder but stop halfway so that your nose is pointing mid-way between the front and the right shoulder. Take a full breath in and as you breathe out allow your head to drop towards the back over your right shoulder. Again, hold this for a full inhalation and exhalation and then gently raise your head. Repeat this to the left.

THE HEART AND LUNGS

This is the area that most people associate with breathing and when we want to take a deep breath the tendency is to heave and expand the upper chest. However, as you have realized by now breathing requires the co-operation of the entire body. Still, this is the area where the atmosphere that has flowed into our lungs meets our blood. The soft, spongy tissues of the lungs are an ideal environment for this exchange of gases and the heart the ideal organ to take this blood and give it a magnificent heave-ho on its journey to the far flung reaches of the body.

This area is also more than that. More than any other area in the body this is an area we protect vigorously. We tense our shoulders and allow this tension to carry down to our arms and hands. We rotate the shoulders forward and tighten up, often looking as if we have taken the chest into retreat. In the course

of checking many people's breathing I have held my hands over breastbones that have felt like solid armour! We even call the wonderful, mobile bones that surround and protect the heart and lungs, the rib *cage*. What is it that we feel will escape or invade?

The hardworking, powerful heart lies snuggled in between the two lungs on either side. In front of it is the sturdy breastbone and behind it the mobile and equally strong thoracic spine. It is this heart that we most closely associate with our feelings of love, compassion, kindness, vulnerability – it is this heart that gets so hurt when any of these, our finest emotions, are rejected or insulted. If the pain that insult to these emotions brings has been felt a few times, we begin to cage the heart in, to build an armour around it, protecting it to protect these, our most tender feelings. Such protection sounds like a good and reasonable idea until you come face to face with the realization that while you are keeping blows out you are also having to keep these emotions in. And these emotions are not meant to be kept in – they are meant to flow freely, like rain and sunshine. When they do flow freely everything softens, the ribs become less like a cage and more like wings, lifting up and away from the sturdy hips that keep us grounded – expanding us outward as well as upward. The arms and hands become instruments of the heart rather than of our bitterness and disappointments.

Try the following awareness techniques:

- Become aware of any holding pattern in your shoulders. Visualize your shoulders widening and consciously allow them to let their weight go.
- Place a hand over your breastbone and feel for any movement.
- Place your hands over your ribs on either side and feel their powerful movement as you breathe.

- Rest your hands on your back and see if you can detect any movement in your thoracic spine as you breathe – can you feel your back widening at all as you breathe in, and contracting as you breathe out?

Here are a few release exercises for this area:

- Take your hands back, opening your chest, and take hold of the chair legs, just below the seat, so that the back of the hands are facing out.
- Breathe in lifting your breast bone – pushing the thoracic vertebrae forward. As you breathe out release. Repeat this three or four times. This exercise stretches the powerful muscles in front of the shoulders and mobilizes the breastbone.
- Breathe in bringing your left arm up over your head, and as you breathe out drop your hand back as if you are holding a tray in the air, at the same time release your shoulder. Then breathe in stretching the heel of your hand upwards towards the ceiling (or towards the sky if you are doing these exercises outdoors). Feel the stretch through the left side of your body. Breathe out releasing the stretch but keeping the arm overhead. Repeat this for three breaths and on the last exhalation slowly lower your arms. Repeat this exercise with your right arm.

THE NAVEL AREA

The navel area really consists of the entire abdomen – the belly. It has been my experience that professionals from Western orthodox medicine, like physiotherapists, will focus on this area in particular when attempting to correct breathing habits. Good breathing to them is abdominal breathing.

Releasing tension from the belly is indeed of vital importance to full and complete breath because only this will allow the diaphragm muscle to descend to its fullest extent. But it is the experience of Yoga teachers, Alexander teachers and a number of other bodywork therapies that focusing on this area and getting the person to 'expand the abdomen' as they breathe in simply serves to increase the tension in the area. It has also been our observation that people are quite capable of breathing poorly – often in a hyperventilating pattern – by using the abdomen. Alan was one such example. The only movement that could be detected when he was breathing was the small in and out movement of his belly.

Reich noticed that there could be rigidity in the rest of the breathing body and over-inflation of the abdomen on inspiration. To Reich this indicated a person who had 'swallowed down' their feelings and was holding them in.

My own experience has led me to believe that too early toilet training can lead to incredible tension in this area and to poor breathing in general. There is evidence that the nerve communication between the brain and the anal sphincter muscle is not complete until the baby is about eighteen months old. Many parents start the toilet training long before this – I have seen mothers begin holding their babies on potties as young as six months. In order to control him or herself before there is control over the anal sphincter muscle, the child has to hold its breath and tighten the muscles of the pelvic floor and the abdomen. This then sets up a habit that the child carries through into adulthood.

What also has to be remembered is that this area also includes the lumbar area of the back where there is often incredible tension. For example, one muscle in this area, the Quadratus Lumborum, is attached to the lower rib and the top of the iliacus (hip) bone at the back. I have often found that this muscle may

be in slight tension, affecting the entire breathing body by distorting it to one side (extreme or chronic tension). Even with mild tightening it prevents the rib from being properly stabilized and the diaphragm therefore fails to descend fully.

The following awareness techniques and exercises are taken from Yoga:

- Remain seated in the chair and place your hands over your navel one hand on top of the other. Feel the movement under your hands and notice whether the belly moves in or out as you breathe in and whether it moves back as you breathe out. The correct movement, the movement in which the diaphragm is able to descend to make space in the thorax for breathing, is for the abdomen to move out on inhalation. Distorted body images fed to us by the media have led many women, in particular, to adopt a habit of holding their bellies in as they try to breathe in. To change this the whole area will have to be softened.

- Drop forward into Forward Sitting Pose. Become aware of the lumbar area of your back. As you breathe focus on this area and see if you can feel the muscles here expanding out to the side as you breathe in and coming back down as you breathe out. When you have connected with this movement sit back up.

- Now place one hand over your navel again and move the other hand to the same position at your back – so that you are in contact with your abdominal area in both the front and back of your body. Feel the movement under your hands and whether there is expansion as you breathe in and contraction as you breathe out.

Now that you have got to know the movement in this area you

can try some ancient Yoga techniques for correcting and releasing breathing. For this exercise you will have to stand up:

- Place your feet about three feet apart with your toes facing 'ten to two' as if you were standing on a big clock, and bend your knees slightly.
- Lean forward and rest your hands on your thighs just above your knees. **Do not allow your shoulders to pull up around your ears.** In order to keep the shoulders in position release your weight down through your legs and into the floor as you also allow your lower back, your tailbone, to release and descend.
- Now breathe in normally letting your abdomen move in whatever direction it is used to. Take your focus to the outbreath. As you breathe out pull your belly inwards and slightly upwards in a powerful contraction that you have taken complete control of. At the same time drop your tailbone further and 'tuck' it under as you arch the lumbar area of your back out. Hold the breath out in this way for just a second and then relax your abdomen and breathe in as you normally do.
- Repeat this three or four times and then take a break.
- Sit back in the chair and place your hands over your abdomen again noticing any changes that have occurred in the movement of your belly.

For the next technique you go onto all fours on the floor, your knees slightly apart, under your hips, and your hands directly under your shoulders, with your fingers slightly splayed. Then do the following simple routine:

- Breathe out and drop your head forward, arch your back up and tuck your tail in. Breathe in lifting your chin and

tail, stretching through the front of your body.

- Repeat this six or seven times.
- Sit back in the chair with your hands over your abdomen and again feel the movement under your hands, noting any changes.
- Sit in Forward Sitting Pose and feel any change in the movement in your back.

THE PELVIC AREA

This is an area of considerable tension for most people – tension brought about by so many things from potty training to sexual anxieties. In Yoga this area is referred to as *kanda*, a Sanskrit word meaning 'root'. This gives us the imagery of the whole pelvic basin as a full, rich bulbous root, connected to the earth and providing nourishment. Housing our reproductive organs, our sexual organs and our organs of elimination, tension in this area can cause wide-ranging problems – including inhibiting the breathing.

The problem is exacerbated in women who may have had long-term pain during menstruation or surgery for caesarean births or hysterectomies. When this has happened the body often adopts a protective muscle tension that continues long after the protection is needed.

The muscles of this area need to be soft, relaxed and welcoming to the descending diaphragm. However in most of us the diaphragm meets enough resistance to arrest its descent.

Try the following awareness exercises:

- Sit in the chair and place your hands over your lower belly. Feel its movement as you breathe. Is there any movement at all? Is it also expanding out with the abdomen or does it remain still?
- Now check your lower back and sitting bones. Is your

back releasing down with the weight falling through the sitting bones, or are you sitting and pulling up your tailbone, creating tension in the lumbar spine?

To begin to release the muscles in this area try the following exercises:

- Lie down on your back on a rug or mat on the floor. Bend your knees and hug both legs into your chest. As you do this feel the whole of your spine coming into contact with the floor and allow your body weight to release through the spine into the floor, through the concrete of the building and into the rich dark earth.
- Release your left leg and slowly straighten it, resting it on the floor while you continue to hug the right leg into your chest.
- Swap over and hug the left leg into your chest having released the right leg.
- Repeat alternating between the left and right leg, holding each leg for about three or four breaths.
- Sit up and bring the soles of your feet together with your knees pointing outward, wrap your hands around your feet. If your hands do not reach use a belt or a scarf.
- Allow your knees to become heavy and relax down.
- Take a deep breath in and raise your knees just a couple of inches. As you breathe out do a gentle whispered 'Ahhhh . . .' letting your knees release down. Be careful not to pull your lower back up during this breathing – let all your weight fall down through your sitting bones.

There is a powerful muscle, called the iliopsoas muscle, that connects the lumbar vertebrae, the front of the hip and the femur (the upper leg bone). I have noticed time and again that if this

muscle is in even a slight contraction it can be felt at the shoulders. Part of the examination of breathing that I do is to place my hands on the person's shoulders to feel the movement of their bodies as they breathe. If I feel that one shoulder is rotating in and down ever so slightly with the exhalation, I will check the opposite iliopsoas muscle – I have yet to find that it is not contracted when I have felt this kind of shoulder activity with breathing. It requires a considerable degree of sensitivity to one's body movements to detect this rotation of the shoulder with the breath. What I advise, because this is such a powerful muscle, is that you do a simple exercise to release and gently stretch it:

- Come up onto your knees and bring your left leg forward placing the foot on the floor. Push the left foot forward so that there is an angle of about 45 degrees between the thigh and the lower leg. Rest your hands on your thigh.
- Breathe in and as you breathe out let your weight slowly sink down so that you feel the gentle stretch up the front of your right thigh. Be careful not to let your body tip forward – if you do that you will lose the stretch.
- Repeat this with the right leg brought forward.

THE LEGS AND FEET

Ill-fitting but highly fashionable shoes often leave our feet distorted and unhappy. One of the first things we do to relax when we come home is kick off our shoes. I remember from growing up in Africa that we ran about barefoot much more than I see children doing in England and Europe. The bare foot is able to splay itself on the ground, making proper contact through which the body can release its weight and renew its vital connection to the earth.

In Greek legend Anteus always regained the strength he had

lost during battle when his body touched the earth – his mother. The hero Hercules noticed this and when it came time for him to do battle against Anteus he picked him up and held him aloft so that the life slowly drained out of him. The buildings we have created, the shoes we constrain our feet in, are gradually making us lose our connection with the earth – which is maybe why so many people are losing vitality. The very best thing you can do is kick off your shoes on a sunny day and walk on the grass, feeling your connection with the earth, allowing the feet to make full contact with the ground and feeling the sense of power that flows up through your body as you walk.

Another tendency of both the rigid body and the collapsed body is to lock the knees back in what is called hyperextension. Contrary to popular belief this is not a straight leg, it is a posture in which the whole body weight falls onto the lower back. In order to allow the weight to fall down through the legs and into the earth, the skin at the back of the knees should be soft. Then it is possible to release the tailbone, soften the buttocks and let the weight fall, going through the feet into the earth.

WHOLE BODY BREATHING

There is an invigorating series of Yoga asanas done in a particular sequence that is called Salute to the Sun. It is usually accompanied by a wonderful chant that begins, "I salute the Sun, the giver of life . . ." Part of this sequence is an excellent way of renewing the contact and communication between all the segments of the body and it is best done before whole body breathing awareness:

- Go onto all fours again on a rug or mat, with your knees slightly apart under the hips and your hands under your shoulders with the fingers slightly splayed. Tuck in your toes.

- Breathe in and as you breathe out drop your knees, chest and chin onto the floor – pushing your buttocks up.
- Breathe in and as you breathe out straighten your legs relaxing your feet and releasing your pelvis and chin so that your whole body is flat on the floor.
- Relax your buttocks and let your pelvis and thighs sink into the floor.
- Breathe in and push up with your arms bringing your head, shoulders and chest off the floor.
- Breathe out and come back up onto all fours and sit back onto your heel, body forward and arms stretched out in Pose of the Moon.
- Repeat this three times and on the last time bring your arms to your side, sliding your hands behind you into the Pose of the Moon.

To be aware of your whole body breathing remain in the Pose of the Moon, placing a folded blanket or towel under your buttocks and a soft covered book under your forehead if that is more comfortable. Then do the following awareness sequence:

- Become aware of your abdomen pushing into your thighs as you breathe in and releasing as you breathe out.
- Become aware of your lower back, the sacrum and the lumbar vertebrae lifting like driftwood on a wave as you breathe in and releasing as you breathe out.
- Become aware of your whole back widening as you breathe in and contracting as you breathe out.
- Become aware of your anus and genitalia gently expanding and opening as you breathe in and contracting lightly as you breathe out.

- Become aware of your whole envelope of skin expanding as you breathe in and contracting as you breathe out.

Try and do this sequence two or three times a week in the beginning as you are trying to change your breathing.

Some frequently asked questions:

Question: I am having difficulty getting my abdomen to move out with my inhalation as it has always moved in on an inhalation. Is there anything else I can do?

Answer: In addition to the above exercises you can try sitting on a chair that has no back, alone, in the centre of a room for a few minutes. Release your weight down through the sitting bones and feet and allow your lower back to drop down without collapsing at the waist. Feel the front and back of the body lengthening and release the muscles at the back of the neck and allow them to lengthen. Let your gaze rest in Tratak on the floor about six or eight feet in front of you. Then take your point of awareness to the ribs at your sides and feel them expanding up and out as you breathe in and come back down as you breathe out. Become aware of the walls of the room on either side of you – their distance from you and the vast space the ribs have to move before they would encounter such an obstacle. This helps them to move even more freely. Become aware of any movement in your back, particularly the lower back behind the abdomen, and as you breathe in feel the space behind your back before it encounters the wall. Hold your focus there for a few moments and then become aware of both the ribs and the back. Finally become aware of the space in front of you. Allow yourself to release the tension in your abdomen and bring to mind all the space in front of the body that the abdomen can expand into without resistance as you breathe in. Then hold your focus on the whole expansion and contraction for a while before you get up and move around. Repeat this four or five

times. This awareness, done over time, will gradually alter the movement of the abdomen.

Question: One way I was shown to breathe abdominally was to lie on my back with a light weight on my stomach that I pushed against. I could not sustain this position because my back hurt after a very short time.

Answer: Precisely, which is why I very seldom use the lying-down-flat-on-the-back technique for breathing awareness. For most people whose lower backs are in a state of tension, this is part of the breathing problem they have and this supine posture simply exaggerates the problem: in this position the lumbar spine is lifted off the floor and tightened, and usually the neck muscles are shortened as the head tilts back. If you do want to lie down and do your breathing use the Alexander Technique position where your knees are bent and your feet are flat on the floor; place a soft covered book about an inch thick under the back of your head so that the muscles at the back of the neck lengthen. Rest your arms on the floor at an angle to your body and rest the palms of your hands on your lower abdomen or pelvis.

There is another reason why I do not as a general rule (there are exceptions to every general rule) do breathing awareness lying down: as soon as you lie down the abdominal cavity responds to gravity by spreading out and invading the thoracic cavity, so the experience of breathing is of shorter breath anyway. We usually lie down to sleep and during sleep breathing is much more shallow as we do not require as much oxygen as when we are up, moving about and therefore using more oxygen.

The system of using resistance to force the abdomen out, which is what you are doing by placing something on your abdomen as you breathe, is not one I use although it is popular among some Yoga teachers. Resistance creates tension –

indeed, all of our tension is about resistance – and there is already an enormous amount of tension in the abdomen and pelvis. There is a natural and wonderful intelligence in the body that knows exactly what to do to breathe fully and completely. In my experience if you remove the layers of tension abdominal breathing restores itself.

Question: I have been suffering from asthma since I was young and I find it very difficult to breathe out completely. Is there any particular exercise I can do?

Answer: Yes, set a candle up about two feet in front of your chair to begin with and have it about two inches below your mouth. Light the candle and breathe out towards the flame through your mouth, making it flicker. You have a definite goal now – to try and make the candle flame flicker for as long as you can without actually blowing it out. As your exhalation becomes more and more powerful you will be able to move the candle further and further away. I have a patient with emphysema who can now keep the candle flickering from four feet away. To achieve this full abdominal breathing needs to be restored.

The other thing you could try if you feel an asthma attack coming is to go down on all fours, knees under the hips and hands under the shoulders, and focus on breathing into your back for a while – take the attention away from the front of your body and breathe into your back.

I use this technique to quickly restore full body breathing if I have been in a stressful situation that has altered my breathing.

The important thing is to become aware of your breathing habits and changes – let your breath be the friend that tells you how you are responding to any given situation.

1. *Dakshina: The Journal of the Traditional Hatha Yoga Association.*

BREATHING
MORE OXYGEN

Hyperbaric Oxygen Therapy can mean the difference between
life and death, coma and non-coma, paralysis and function.

DR R. A. NEUBAUER

Hyperbaric Oxygen Therapy – breathing a higher concentration of oxygen under pressure – is emerging as a significant 'new' therapy for a number of acute and chronic conditions, including multiple sclerosis, chronic fatigue syndrome, wound healing, stroke symptoms, treatment of AIDS and even for infants disabled by deprivation of oxygen at birth. It is also being advocated for use in acute and chronic infections, burns, bone disorders (such as fractures that will not heal), and circulatory problems, including those brought about through Diabetes. It is my belief that as we move into the new century this therapy will gain more and more ground and that Hyperbaric Oxygen Therapy will be a vital part of twenty-first century medicine.

Hyperbaric simply means pressure greater than sea-level atmospheric pressure. How is breathing oxygen under greater pressure different? In a sense we are already breathing under pressure. If you remember in Chapter Two we talked about atmospheric pressure and the partial pressure of different gases. We also saw that the transport of air into and out of the lungs in the thoracic cavity, the arteries and even the cells of our body via the bloodstream, are all subject to the law which governs the movement of gases – gas molecules always move *down* a pressure gradient. Any change in atmospheric pressure therefore alters the amount of oxygen absorbed into the body.

The higher up we go the more atmospheric pressure decreases. I was born in Johannesburg – a giddy 6000ft above sea-level – and whenever I visit this city of my birth I am at a higher altitude than when I am at home in Berkshire, England (which is practically at sea level). The effect of this is that I tire more easily in Johannesburg than I do in Berkshire, and I'm much less likely to be able to run up a flight of stairs there without becoming breathless. When you travel from sea-level to a high-altitude you are moving from an area of high atmospheric pressure to an area of low atmospheric pressure: the higher the altitude the lower the atmospheric pressure. This means the partial pressure of oxygen in the atmosphere will also be lower as will oxygen density. As I go higher up not only is there a decrease in pressure forcing less air into my lungs, there is a decrease in the oxygen available in the air.

People who live at high altitudes – and therefore lower atmospheric pressure – have more red blood cells to transport oxygen, more capillaries in the brain, slightly enlarged hearts to circulate that oxygen more rapidly, and they tend to breathe more deeply. When you travel quickly from high atmospheric pressure to low atmospheric pressure you can suffer from breathlessness, dizziness, fatigue and even nausea. This is a common problem for people going from their homes at sea-level to ski resorts high in the mountains for their holidays, it is called *acute mountain sickness* (AMS). Fortunately for the body, knowing fully its complete dependence on oxygen, the symptoms only last for a few days – full acclimatization takes about three weeks. Another quick look at atmospheric pressure and

PRINCIPLES OF BREATHWORK

internal respiration will explain why these changes happen and what happens when you reverse this process and *increase* the pressure, which is the key to understanding how hyperbaric oxygen therapy works.

MEASURING ATMOSPHERIC PRESSURE

Scientists generally measure atmospheric pressure in terms of mercury because mercury is a relatively heavy substance so the column to hold it as it rises will not have to be exceptionally tall. The pressure of 15 pounds per square inch of atmospheric pressure is enough to raise a column of mercury 760mm in the air (nearly 30 inches). This is expressed as 760mm Hg (mm = millimetres; Hg is the abbreviation for mercury). The atmospheric pressure at sea-level is 760mm Hg. Oxygen only makes up about 21 per cent of this atmosphere so it exerts a partial pressure of 159mm Hg.

A drop or an increase in the atmospheric pressure as we breathe impacts on our internal respiration. During Hyperbaric Oxygen Therapy the pressure is increased only slightly – to 1, 1.75, or 2 times atmospheric pressure – yet the benefits are dramatic. This benefit is largely due to the change in the transportation of oxygen from the lungs to the cells of the body.

Breathing deeply and in excess of your metabolic requirements under normal atmospheric conditions is not going to significantly improve the delivery of oxygen to the tissues and cells of your body. Allowing your body to release muscles and experience its full and proper breathing cycle returns it to a rhythm that is not interfered with or altered by chronic tension. Calm and relaxed breathing in which the muscles participate as they should rather than being bound and inhibiting breathing, means that the body is more easily able to regulate its oxygen/carbon dioxide levels to its needs. As we have seen in the previous chapters 'deep breathing' will in fact simply lower the levels of carbon dioxide and eventually lead to breathing problems. However, in chronic illnesses like those mentioned above where cells have deteriorated or died due to lack of oxygen, delivering oxygen up to the normal values of cells leads to healing and an acceleration of the healing process. A safe way of delivering more oxygen to cells without upsetting the oxygen/carbon dioxide balance is through the use of hyperbaric atmospheric conditions and this is known as *Hyperbaric Oxygen Therapy*.

THE OXYGEN TWO-STEP

The small but innumerable rivers of blood returning to the lungs after they have delivered oxygen to the cells of the body, still have a considerable amount of oxygen in them. However the blood will have delivered enough oxygen to have a lower partial pressure than the air in the alveoli of the lungs, so oxygen will move from the lungs into the blood.

What we call blood flowing through these capillaries is actually made up of a liquid called plasma, in which the red and (many fewer) white blood cells are suspended. Plasma is by far the most plentiful substance flowing through our arteries and veins but it is the red blood cells that take up most inhaled oxygen to ferry it through the body. Red blood cells, shaped like bi-concave discs with a hollowed centre, carry within themselves haemoglobin. They have wonderful flexibility and are able to deform themselves as they move through capillaries that are much smaller than they are. Each haemoglobin can combine with four molecules of oxygen. This is a much better pick up rate than water, for example, and a teaspoon full of red blood cells is able to carry about 60 times as much oxygen as a teaspoon full of water. When oxygen has combined with

haemoglobin it becomes oxyhaemoglobin. The plasma, more plentiful than red blood cells, does pick up some oxygen but not much because 90 per cent of its volume is made up of water and water is less efficient than haemoglobin at taking it up.

Once oxygen has made the step from the lungs into the haemoglobin it has hitched its ride through the body but it cannot 'unbind' itself from the haemoglobin and move straight into a cell. Instead it is a two-step move: first from the haemoglobin into the plasma (where it dissolves to become 'free' oxygen) and then into the cells. A number of factors cause this unbinding of oxygen to accelerate by the time the blood reaches the systemic capillaries, where it is in most direct contact with the cells of the body, and a rapid exchange of oxygen and carbon dioxide takes place. Because of this two-step movement, however, oxygen could be more efficiently delivered to body cells if there were more of it available in the plasma to begin with.

When you go to a high altitude where less oxygen is available at less pressure, the net result is that there is less oxygen entering the lungs to be taken up by the blood. Because oxygen provides us with energy the first thing we will notice is that we have less. This is why on the first few days in Johannesburg when I visit I'm always too tired to engage in the hectic programme of activities lined up by friends and family.

TAKING THE PRESSURE: HYPERBARIC OXYGEN THERAPY

The reverse of going up to dizzy heights and lower pressures is, of course, to go downward to *increased* atmospheric pressure.

If you go diving you increase the pressure weighing down on you. This is calculated by taking into account the pressure of the air above the water and the weight of the water (water is heavier than air). For every 33 feet a diver descends you can add 1 atmospheric unit of pressure, so air is entering the lungs, and the cells of the body, at greater than normal pressure.

This has the opposite effect of mountain climbing. Even if the gas tank of the diver contains the same percentage of oxygen as the atmosphere on land, the partial pressure is increased and a greater quantity of oxygen will be taken into the arteries because of this increased pressure. Oxygen will enter **not only the red blood cells containing haemoglobin, but it will also be forced into the plasma which is much more abundant than red blood cells**. This plasma, now containing greater concentration of oxygen, will move into the body. The increased pressure will move this oxygen into tissues to a much greater extent than under normal atmospheric conditions. Oxygen will then easily diffuse directly into tissue cells, seeping even further than those cells not directly in contact with capillaries. This oxygen can enter areas of tissue where circulation has been blocked or impaired, and relieve oxygen deprivation of the cells. This availability of oxygen allows the body to grow new capillaries to replace any that have been damaged or destroyed. This is why Hyperbaric Oxygen Therapy is also being used for circulatory disease problems which are a consequence of diabetes or atherosclerosis which is an accumulation of fatty deposits on the artery walls.

Because oxygen is our 'life-giving and life-sustaining' ingredient this added oxygen enables the repair of damaged tissue. In the first chapter of this book we saw how we evolved in the presence of oxygen and how that presence created beings of enormous complexity. That complexity continues to be served by oxygen and no life or healing can take place without it. Let us look at just one disease where hyperbaric oxygen has been found to alleviate and sometimes arrest symptoms, in patients with Multiple Sclerosis.

HYPERBARIC OXYGEN THERAPY AND MULTIPLE SCLEROSIS

In the UK, many sufferers of Multiple Sclerosis (MS) use Hyperbaric Oxygen Therapy to help alleviate the symptoms of this disease, although this therapy is not supplied by the National Health Service. MS patients themselves have organized centres where they can go and receive more oxygen through Hyperbaric Oxygen Therapy and other therapies. The fact that these units have continued and increased over the years speaks highly of the effectiveness of this therapy – despite the fact that most GPs and neurologists (usually the specialists attending MS sufferers) are unaware of its benefits.

Multiple Sclerosis means 'many scars', and it describes the symptoms of MS rather than the disease itself. Nerves carry signals throughout the body – from the brain to the muscles, heart, lungs, kidneys, etc., and from the body back to the brain. If we touch something hot the nerve fibres send a message to the brain conveying all the information the brain needs about the intensity and proximity of the heat; the brain then sends a message to the muscle to pull the hand back – before we have even 'registered' that the surface is hot. Some of these vital nerve fibres are covered by a *myelin sheath* to increase the speed of conduction of the messages travelling along them – other fibres are not myelinated. The 'many scars' referred to in Multiple Sclerosis is where damage has occurred to this myelin sheath and to the nerve fibres themselves. As the body attempts to heal damage made to the nerve it creates a plaque, or scar, at the site of the damage. In a typical area of damage in MS both the mylin sheath and the nerve fibre may be damaged or destroyed. The result is that messages from and to other parts of the brain are greatly impaired, resulting in loss of use of muscles, sometimes loss of sight and as the disease progresses, loss of voice and even ability to breathe independently. However, MS usually appears in a kind of relapse-and-remission pattern. During the period of remission symptoms improve even if they do not entirely disappear. During relapse the disease becomes active and symptoms that disappeared during remission return or prevailing symptoms intensify.

It would appear that most MS research concentrates on finding a way to repair or regenerate the myelin sheath. Unfortunately, the nerve fibres themselves also deteriorate and therefore some specialists like Dr James say much of the current research is misguided. In a convincing paper published in the Lancet (the most prominent medical journal in the world) in 1982 (February 13th issue) Dr James discussed the background to the mechanisms of blood vessel involvement in MS. Dr James says that since the use of MRI (Magnetic Resonance Image) scanning new information has come to light which disproves many of the old theories about MS. Despite this, the continued concentration on myelin, for whatever reasons, has diverted the attention of doctors from blood vessel abnormalities.

We do know that a number of body systems other than the nervous system are involved in the disease. For example, MS appears also to be a vascular disease because MRI scanning indicates that tiny blood vessels in the central nervous system of MS patients show leakage, which can lead to damaging the extremely sensitive nerve tissue and the myelin sheath in the brain and/or spinal cord. The sensible thing, then, would be to deliver such treatment as would heal the damaged blood vessels as quickly as possible in order to prevent further damage to nerve tissue. That is where Hyperbaric Oxygen Therapy has such a part to play because, as Dr James writes:

> The objective for any therapy introduced in the established disease is to stabilize the patient or, in other words, to induce the best possible remission. The disease process must be limited

before scarring takes place. What is the most crucial substance to the induction of remission or healing? – Oxygen.[1]

Sufficient oxygen delivered under pressure greater than atmospheric pressure can allow the rapid return of the affected area to normal, so that damage to myelin and nerve fibres does not occur. The scars that occur on the myelin sheath are the body's way of repairing and healing the damage itself and that cannot be reversed.

Dr James calls oxygen the 'orphan drug'. Let us hope that those thousands of people suffering from diseases like Multiple Sclerosis who have been helped by Hyperbaric Oxygen Therapy, will lead the way and that the rest of us will realize the healing benefits of this colourless, odourless, life-giving gas – which is still free!

We should not wait for the medical profession to deliver it to us either. There are many reasons why this may not happen: chiefly the fact that it is not a drug that is being marketed. Like MS sufferers we should all investigate the research and organize ourselves to ensure its availability. I was delighted to see on the television news recently an item about a mother who started The Hyperbaric Oxygen Trust in East Grinstead after organizing this for her own child.

As Dr James says:

What is the final message?

... it is simply keep breathing, it makes you feel better;

and breathe more oxygen when you are ill and you will get better faster.

It is improving on nature.

1. Philip James PhD, FFOM. Hyperbaric Oxygen Therapy for Multiple Sclerosis Patients: Where Are We Now? *The Lancet*, 13 February 1982.

THE SOUL
OF BREATHING

Even the gods breathe along with the breath
As does man and beast.
For truly, breath is the life of all beings; the Life of
all life.
To a full life go they
Who worship God as breath.
For truly, breath is the life of all beings; the Life of all life.

TAITTIRIYA UPANISHAD 2:3

At the heart of the spiritual teachings of the most ancient cultures of the earth we find breathwork. To the Tantrics and Yogis of India, the spiritual teachers of China that came from both Daoism and later Buddhism, and the Zen masters of Japan, enlightenment was the natural culmination of every life and every being would inevitably pursue this enlightenment, regardless of their history or other predispositions. All these teachings hold unequivocally that a knowledge of self had to be gained for enlightenment to happen, and that the only means of gaining such self-knowledge is by turning the vision inwards. The path that vision must then follow is the path of the breath. This is most beautifully stated by the Vietnamese Buddhist monk, the Reverend Thich Nhat Hanh:

Breathing and knowing that we are breathing is a basic practice. No one can be truly successful in the art of meditating without going through the door of breathing. To practice conscious breathing is to open the door to *stopping* and *looking deeply* in order to enter the domain of concentration and insight . . . Conscious breathing is the way into any sort of meditative concentration.[1]

We will look at some aspects of each of these – Yoga, Daoism and Zen, with a special emphasis on Yoga as it remains the most common contact we in the West have with a system that incorporates breathwork in a spiritual context as well as a physical one.

THE MOST ANCIENT AMONG THE ANCIENTS

At the dawn of human consciousness, before the thinkers, philosophers and playwrights of Greece and even before the mighty pyramids of Egypt and the Sphinx of Giza, an inspiring philosophy with a practical application emerged in India. We have come to know this philosophy as Tantra. Tantra covered every field of human endeavour from agriculture and winemaking to medicine and spiritual enlightenment. The Tantrics were builders and mathematicians, artists and farmers, doctors and saints. They gave to the world the zero to which the great mathematicians of Greece owe their fame. It was as if we, as humans beings, gathered in that place and time to distil wisdom that we could spread through all the populations of humankind to provide nourishment and knowledge to last us through the coming centuries.

Essentially a 'how to' philosophy, a guide to action springing from enquiry, Tantra was to lose its vitality as society in India reorganized itself into the caste system. Just as Greek society was to do many years later, Indian society became organized on the basis of a separation of 'knowledge' and 'labour'. Worldly knowledge and work became the province of those with the least social status, while those with 'spiritual' knowledge lived off the surplus produced by them. Plato was to echo this in Greece with his *Laws* in which he describes the organization of society on the basis of slavery:

> We have now made excellent arrangements to free our citizens from the necessity of manual labour; the business of the arts and crafts have been passed onto others; agriculture has been handed over to slaves on condition of their granting us a sufficient return to live in a fit and seemly fashion . . .

Thus the stage was set for knowledge gained through an enquiry into nature to be viewed with contempt. While that contempt would survive in Western culture until the 1500s when Descarte elevated the study of nature to that of a worthy pursuit. By the early eighteenth century medicine underwent a dramatic change that allowed for an examination of the human body that had been forbidden before but, as we saw in Chapter Four, this led to another kind of separation. In India the Tantric system never went away – it changed form to survive. Tantra continued through the philosophies and practical applications of Yoga and other belief systems like Shaivism. Buddhism, which was born out of Hinduism, at first violently opposed Tantra, but later came to adopt many of its esoteric and sacred texts and rituals as its own – spreading them to China, Japan and Tibet (and in this century to the West, where it is one of the fastest growing religions). The most direct descendent of Tantra that we have, however, is Yoga. Most surviving tantric texts can be divided into four parts, *jnana* (knowledge), *yoga* (focus),

kriya (action), and *carya* (conduct). It is here that breathing is explored in awe-inspiring depth as the tantrics sought knowledge about themselves and their relationship with the world.

THE ESSENTIAL VITALITY

To the Yogis breath is much more than the inhalation of oxygen and the exhalation of carbon dioxide. To the Yogi breath is *prana* – the essential vitality that all life is dependent upon. This prana precedes creation and all creation issues from it. It is not a hierarchy: biology is not subordinate to prana even while it is dependent on it – it is prana made manifest. This whole universe of multiple galaxies and burning suns, as well as you and I and all of nature on our planet, are manifestations of prana. *Prana is the life-force of all things: the exuberance and vitality behind all life and permeating all life.* The word prana is derived from one of the root verbs of Sanskrit, 'pri' – to fill. The added affix 'na' means it can be used in either the active or passive voice. It can be translated as breath, power, vitality or even spirit. To the ancients these were not separate: without breath there could be no power, no vitality, no spiritual pathway.

Prana is divided into five distinct parts, but we will be looking at just three:

- the inhalation, *prana*, the beginning, the taking in of vitality and nourishment from the environment;
- the exhalation, *apana*, the release of breath once the vital prana has been absorbed;
- the all pervading, *vyana*, the prana pervading the body through internal respiration.

These three parts of prana reflect the phases of the energy of expansion, contraction and equilibrium which we covered earlier. They refer not only to the act of breathing but to the movement of prana as a whole. Consciousness of the movement of prana is gained through conscious breathing which acts as the wind that picks up our awareness and carries it into a self filled with potential and possibilities, a self where prana is as real as the blood flowing through our veins and where we are able to see ourselves reflected in the universe around us.

PRANA AND LIBIDO

Behind material form and function, the Yogis say, a vibrant pranic body operates and by its operation the material world comes into being, renews itself and eventually dissolves back into the elements. The human body, along with all of manifest creation, emerges from that all-pervasive pranic vibration. Usually at this point when writers discuss prana or life-force they introduce the ancient Greeks as another example of a people who had a belief in a life-force. However, when we do this we are likely to conclude that it is an old idea and that we must have had some new and better ideas since then – that perhaps the prana or 'life-force' theory is simply a peculiarity of our ancient history that we should move beyond. But I think it is much more recent in our Western history than we think.

In the Judeo/Christian book of origin, Genesis, man was said to be made from clay – and woman then fashioned from man. Thus, to describe our origins the West had looked to the technology then at its disposal, pottery. Steven Rose, biologist and scientist, says in his introduction to the recently published, *The First Book of Moses, Called Genesis*:

> Making objects from clay was one of the first human technologies and analogising the act of human creation to that of the potter begins a tradition of attempting to understand living processes via technological artifacts which continues today. A modern-day

God would perhaps take a computer and breathe consciousness into it.

Here we see that breath is that which gives life to the fashioned object and the human form is a reflection of the available technology.

To Newton the body came to reflect the foremost technology of his time – the clock with working parts – each of which could be precisely measured. A famous French psychoanalyst Jaques Lacan was to say of this view that it took the life out of biology and that it bound biologists to the perspectives of the mechanic who, like Descartes and Newton, '. . . searched in the body for the machine'.

Lacan also said that while the invention of the machine removed the study of life from biology it allowed us to examine something that had not been examined before, namely energy – and the effects of energy on the human body. This, Lacan said, is what Freud did. To Freud biology was not the biology of the mechanic but rather the movement of energy in the human body and what that movement symbolised. Freud was to call this energy *libido*. Exactly the same thing can be said of prana – its study is the study of the disposition of energy in human functioning.

In fact, neither libido nor prana can strictly be translated as energy because energy requires some means of measurement. We are unable to say, for example, that it takes X amount of prana or libido to push a book six inches across the table. Rather, prana and libido are measured by observing their manifestations, their 'disposition in human functioning'.

To Freud libido, in the process of our human development, was withdrawn from other bodily functions and organized under the primacy of the genitalia. To the Yogis prana is organized, through the breath, under the primacy of the *panchatattva* – the five thatnesses.

It is incredibly difficult, having spent so much time thinking of ourselves as being something like a machine – and now like a *computer* machine – to see ourselves reflected not in machinery, but in nature. The basic challenge to machine-mindedness is breathing. Machines do not breathe. We, however, like all of the rest of nature, do. So the Yogis saw us reflected in nature around us. For example, they looked at the rich dark earth which supports this evolving life-force, at its valleys of abundance, its solid mountains, its rich plains and they said 'Ah, we too have that within us.' We have the power of support, solidity and cohesion. We have bones that are solid, that give our soft tissue support and cohesion. The body holds itself together as nature operating through the body offers support and help to others. Those properties of the earth are reflected in us also and we therefore have a quality, a thatness, of the earth. The word *tattva* literally means thatness, and they named and described five (*pancha*) of them: *prithvi* (earth), *apas* (water), *agni* (fire), *vayu* (air), *akasha* (space). Prana, they said, is organized by these tattva within us, each of which has a specific place of focus within the pranic being.

Like the meridians of Chinese medicine, from these points of focus the prana, taken in through the breath and organized by these tattvas, would be carried throughout the body. The points of focus themselves are situated in the major meridian of the body called Sushumna – the Shining Pathway – that stretches along the whole length of the spine and beyond it. Each tattva takes the prana of the breath and imbues it with its own special vitality.

PRITHVI – THE EARTH

Prithvi, the earth focus, is situated at the perineum between the anus and the genitalia – literally where your body meets the ground if you sit on it. Breath reaching there is transformed into the vitality that gives stability, support, cohesion – physically and psychologically. If a bone is broken it is through the vitality of prithvi, which means 'to be', that it will knit together. Through the power of prithvi we will feel grounded, secure, with a sense of belonging. It governs our sense of smell. If this prana is disturbed we will lose our balance, our ability to walk our own way. We will have confusion about our purpose. Physically we will lose bone mass – as in old age when this prana begins to withdraw. Those in whom this focus is strong are usually well-built, solid, giving, non-judgemental, supportive people. If this focus is strong and has become unbalanced they can more easily than others become stuck and rigid.

APAS – WATER

Apas, which means to pervade, has its focus situated at the base of the spine. It transforms breath into the vitality that imparts the ability to create. It therefore gives us our sexual potency as well as our reproductive capacities. We develop within the watery wombs of our mothers – our first environment – before we step onto earth. Our ability to create is not confined to our sexuality – we create and recreate ourselves in many ways: the artist, the writer, the gardener, the scientist, are all using their creative abilities provided by apas tattva. When this tattva is disturbed we lose that ability – we lose the capacity to dive deep within ourselves to access the creative power of water. This water is also said to be our ancient memory – the genetic pattern – that carries within it the entire history of creation. People in whom this focus is strongest are usually deep thinkers and philosophers. When it becomes unbalanced however, they can become morose, depressed and uncommunicative.

Agni is our capacity for transformation – we breathe in oxygen
and transform it through our own alchemy into something else.
We eat food and transform it into molecules our body can use.
More than any other tattva Agni gives us our personal ambience
– the quality that people can feel and are aware of long before
we speak to each other. It is also that ability to transform ideas
and information into that which we can use. People in whom
this tattva is strong will be the 'rainmakers' in our society – they
will always have the ability to transform. These are the people
who change the whole atmosphere in a room by just walking in,
who always have a crowd around them at a party and who can
sell you ice in winter. Situated behind the navel Agni also governs our sense of sight and our vision for ourselves. Unbalanced
it can mean highs and lows – as in manic depression.

VAYU – AIR

Vayu also means wind. Situated behind the heart this focus
gives prana its capacity for movement, just like the wind,
another translation of vayu. This movement of prana, transformed by the tattvas, throughout our body is under the gover-
norship of vayu. We can see each tattva expressed in each cell:
each cell has cohesion (earth), has the capacity to recreate itself
(water), to transform nutrients into energy (fire), to move
(vayu), and to organize itself (akasha). Vayu is also our capacity
of movement in the world we are born into – the grace and fluidity with which we move through that world. It is also the
movement of thought – the quickness of our ideas. It governs
our sense of touch – our sensory awareness – as well as our
ability to be touched. Those in whom this focus is strongest will
display great leadership qualities with the courage to act on
their ideas. When this tattva becomes unbalanced we may
become impulsive and reckless.

AKASHA – SPACE

The last of the five tattvas, situated at the base of the throat, is akasha – space. This is the beginning of creation, the ability to make order out of chaos. It is the Big Bang becoming galaxies and solar systems. This is prana converted into the capacity to sustain and organize the instructions held in the DNA and RNA in order that it can continue to know its function. Akasha governs our sense of hearing and our capacity to speak with our own voice. Those in whom this tattva is strongest have great organizational abilities – everything in their home or work environment will have a place and be in its place. When this tattva loses its vitality we lose the capacity to organize ourselves meaningfully and properly. We lose creative routine just as the cells of our body lose track of their instructions. Or conversely we can become obsessed with routine and tidiness.

PRANA AND THE PANCHATATTVA

There is a great Tantric text that begins with a request from the goddess Shakti to the god Siva:

> Great One, I beseech you, give me that knowledge by which I may become perfect.

And he replies:

> Through knowledge of the tattvas perfection is achieved.

The rest of this text goes on to give instructions on breathing as the means of both accessing and balancing each of these tattvas.

BREATH AND THE TATTVAS

Each tattva receives its vitality from the breath. Modern, shallow, hyperventilating breathing hardly feeds and nourishes

these tattvas at all. People are left feeling exhausted, dispirited, lost, as each tattva loses contact with the breath. A survey of doctors reported the most common syndrome people came to see them about was TATT – Tired All The Time! This is not surprising considering we do not nourish this deep pranic self – that we do not usually even have any knowledge of it. There is a natural withdrawal of the prana towards the end of a person's life – our problem is that we are living that way for forty, fifty and sometimes sixty years, never achieving our full potential.

The tattvas are also under the influence of expansion, contraction and equilibrium. The Fire and Air tattvas must expand during the day and calm down at night when the Water and Earth tattvas expand and so on. The way we ensure that this rhythm is maintained is through the three phases of pranic breathing: prana (complete, conscious inhalation), apana (complete, conscious exhalation) and vyana (complete conscious diffusion). Ways of doing this will be covered in the next chapter.

QI: THE MOVEMENT EAST – AND WEST

QI IN CHINA

The Chinese have long held that there is a fundamental life-force, just as the Yogis and Tantrics did. They call it Qi (pronounced Chee). Although Chinese medicine associates Qi much more closely with the blood than the breath, in Chinese bodywork systems like Qi Gong and martial arts like Tai Chi and Kung Fu, Qi is accessed through voice and breath.

Acupuncture, a branch of Chinese medicine, is entirely devoted to re-establishing the balance of Qi in the meridians of the body by inserting a fine needle into specific points along these meridians. As with the Yogis, disease is seen as a manifestation of an imbalance in this life-force. Even in the canons of acupuncture, breathing is both a means of 'reading' the state of

Qi and of transforming it. Chinese medicine holds that there are three areas in the body of particular importance: the three dantians. The lower dantian is the area just below the navel; the middle dantian is the area of the chest in front of the heart; and the upper dantian is the space between the eyebrows. These dantian are energetic centres which store and transform Qi. In most Daoist contemplative breathing practices breath is directed and circulated through these dantian.

KI IN JAPAN

In Japan the life-force is called Ki. Ki corresponds exactly to the Chinese Qi. In Zen Buddhism, which is widely practised in Japan, breath again plays a vital role in spiritual enlightenment and energetic balance. Breathing, with movement, is seen as one of the basic methods of directing Ki.

BREATHING IN MEDITATIVE PRACTICES

Enlightenment, from an Eastern perspective, does not happen without the body. It is not something to look forward to after death – it is something we begin to walk towards as embodied beings. Breath is the vital link between inner and outer; up and down; ignorance and enlightenment. This can be stated in the most simple but powerful way, as the Reverend Thich Nhat Hanh advises:

Breathing in, I know I am breathing in,
Breathing out, I know I am breathing out.

1. Thich Nhat Hanh. *The Blooming of a Lotus*, Thich Nhat Hanh (see Resources).

BREATHING LIFE INTO LIFE

The body's respiration is one constant process between life and death, regardless of the span of time. The infant becomes a developing child; the youth will become old. The body may become diseased or distorted; joyfulness may be displaced by agony or vacant awareness. Throughout each life, both desirable and undesirable events will usher in change, but breath will be a continuing part of that life . . . As breathing goes on whether one is aware of it or not, the breath is always available to use as a device for meditation focus.

R.W. BOERSTLER AND H.S. KORNFELD

There are extremely powerful breathing techniques which not only balance the vitality and allow it to flow freely through the body, but which quiet the mind and prepare it for self awareness and meditation.

I suggest that you try the exercises in Chapter Five before you begin these, as a body that is relatively free of tension is a better meditating tool than one in which tension is still firmly fixed.

EXERCISE ONE: CONNECTING WITH THE PHYSICAL SELF

This exercise allows you to become aware of and connect, via the breath, with your inner physical self. It is taken from an ancient Daoist practice which has been modified slightly for use in the West. Sit in a position that is comfortable, in which your back has support and in an environment that feels warm and safe. Then after you have read through the steps of the exercise, close your eyes and try to visualize the whole sequence.

- *Step One:* Become aware of the flow of breath in and out of your body. You are not trying to breathe deeply – you are simply watching your breath with curiosity, its coming and going.
- *Step Two:* Become aware of the moment between breaths, the still-point of the body when it balances its needs with the needs of the environment. Enter into the still-point as deeply as you are able – seeking out in it the moment when the next inhalation begins and the place it begins from. (*Note:* All the breathing and meditation sequences begin with these two steps.)
- *Step Three:* Visualize your whole skeleton: the cranial vault that protects and holds your brain, the entire length of the spine, the ribs, the long bones of the arms and hands, the hips and the long bones of the legs and feet.
- *Step Four:* Breathe in feeling that the prana/qi from the breath enters your lungs with the breath, as the 'breath within the breath' of Rumi, the poet. As you exhale this prana is carried throughout the length of the skeleton and wraps around it. During that brief still-point visualize this prana penetrating the skeleton. Repeat this process for three rounds of inhalation, exhalation and still-point.

- *Step Five:* Visualize your major internal organs: Your heart, your lungs, your stomach, spleen, intestines, kidneys, liver, or choose just one of the major organs – perhaps one that has become weak. So, if you are suffering from high blood pressure, picture the heart and the rich flow of blood through the entire body. If you suffer from disturbed digestion or malabsorption choose the stomach and intestines, and so on.

- *Step Six:* Breathe in feeling the prana/qi from the breath enter your lungs with the breath, as the 'breath within the breath' of Rumi the poet. As your body breathes out feel that the prana/qi gathered during that in-breath is travelling though the body and wrapping around the organs or single organ. During the brief still-point allow this prana/qi to penetrate the organs you are holding in your visualization. Repeat this process for three more rounds of in-breath, out-breath and still-point.

- *Step Seven*: Visualize the musculature of your body. You do not need to know the placement of each and every muscle – simply be aware of the sheet of muscle tissue that surrounds your entire frame and is responsible for 'moving' your breath and moving you wherever you want to go.

- *Step Eight*: Breathe in, feeling that the prana/qi from the breath enters your lungs with the breath, as the 'breath within the breath' of Rumi, the poet. As you breathe out feel the prana/qi gathered from the in-breath flowing throughout the musculature of the body and wrapping itself around it. During the brief still-point feel the prana/qi penetrate the muscles of your whole body. Repeat this process for three more rounds of in-breath, out-breath and still-point.

- *Step Nine:* Visualize your whole body, from the top of your head down to the tips of your fingers and toes – the whole space that you occupy.
- *Step Ten:* Breathe in feeling that the prana/qi from the breath enters your lungs with the breath, as the 'breath within the breath' of Rumi, the poet. As you breathe out feel that the prana/qi gathered during the in-breath has wrapped itself around your whole body. During the brief moment of the still-point allow this prana to deeply enter and penetrate your whole being. Repeat this process for three more rounds of inhalation, exhalation and still-point.

You can allow this exercise to be as complex or as simple as you like. There may be some problem you are experiencing and then you can focus on that area. For example, a patient who used to experience terrible pain during her periods every month when she was a teenager used this breathing technique to visualize the prana/qi entering her uterus and calming it down. Some of my patients with Multiple Sclerosis visualize their brain and spinal cord and allow the prana/qi to penetrate those. Alan used it to visualize the prana/qi penetrating his whole circulatory system. I always advise that you finish with the 'whole body' breath to keep in mind your wholeness – otherwise it is very easy to become identified with just one part of one's self – usually the part that is not working well.

EXERCISE TWO: CONNECTING WITH THE PRANIC SELF

In this exercise we connect with the points of focus of each tattva and allow the breath to penetrate them, invigorate them and balance them. Again read through the steps and then take a comfortable, supported seat and allow your breath and mind to work in harmonized focus.

- *Step One*: Become aware of the tide of air flowing in and out of your body. Feel its rhythm and be particularly aware of the coolness of the breath as it enters your nose, hits the back of your throat and then enters your lungs. As you exhale become aware that the breath leaving your lungs feels warm as it rises up your throat and leaves through your nose. Be aware of the still-point and the beginning of all breath within it.
- *Step Two:* Visualize a radiant hollow tube running from the crown of your head, down your spine, emerging from the base of your spine and continuing down to the perineum. As you breathe in visualize a cool current flowing down this radiant tube, and as you breathe out feel a warm current rising up it. During the still-point visualize the radiance of the tube growing ever brighter. Repeat this three times.
- *Step Three:* At the perineum visualize a yellow square that holds the same power as that of the earth: support, stability, cohesion. As you breathe in allow the cool current generated by the in-breath to connect with that square and flood into it. As you breathe out allow the warm current to flow from the square, drawing its energy up to the base of the spine. During the still-point feel that the many small currents flowing from this focus of energy are open and receptive to this renewed 'earth' energy.
- *Step Four:* This energy of the earth now connects with the base of the spine, the place of focus of water tattva. Visualize the shape of a silvery crescent moon on a dark blue background and that this shape holds the qualities of water – creativity, will and memory. Breathe in and let the

cool current strike open this point of energy and flow into it. As you breathe out allow the warm current to flow up from this crescent shape and connect with the place behind the navel. During the still-point feel that the many small currents flowing from this focus of energy are open and receptive to this renewed 'water' energy.

- *Step Five:* Now both the earth and water energy have connected to the fire energy behind the navel. Become aware of a fiery triangle with its apex pointed downward – holding the power of transformation and vision. Allow the cool current going down the radiant hollow tube to strike this point of energy, open it, and flow into it as you breathe in. As you breathe out feel the warm current rising and connecting with the point behind the heart. During the still-point feel that the many small currents flowing from this focus of energy are open and receptive to this renewed 'fire' energy.

- *Step Six:* The energies of earth, water and fire have now connected with the energy of air, in the radiant hollow tube behind the heart. Visualize a smoky hexagonal shape in this space carrying the power of air – movement, sensitivity, motivation and lightness of being. As you breathe in allow the cool current flowing down the tube to open this point of energy and flow in. As you breathe out let the warm current rise up the tube to the base of the back of the neck. During the still-point feel that the many small currents flowing from this focus of energy are open and receptive to this renewed 'air' energy.

- *Step Six*: The energies of earth, water, fire and air have now been connected with the energy of space at the base of the neck. Visualize a white full moon shape at this point holding the energy of organization, order and manifestation. As you breathe in allow the cool current to open this energy point and feel the prana flow in. As you breathe out allow the warm current to rise to the point between your eyebrows. During the still-point feel that the many small currents flowing from this focus of energy are open and receptive to this renewed 'space' energy.

- *Step Seven*: Now the energies of earth, water, fire, air and space have been drawn to the space between the eyebrows. This particular point is their centre for balance. Breathe into this centre between the eyebrows. Feel it drawing the prana to balance and energise each of these tattvas it is now holding. As you breathe out feel that each tattva is released back down into its focus of energy along the radiant tube. Breathe in and out five times and with each exhalation let one energy return to its base: feel the space energy return to the full moon at the base of the neck, renewed, balanced, invigorated; the air energy returns to the hexagon behind the heart renewed, balanced and invigorated; the fire energy returns to the fiery triangle with its apex pointed downward renewed, balanced and invigorated; the water energy returns to the crescent moon on the dark back-ground renewed, balanced and invigorated; and finally the earth energy returns to the square at the perineum also renewed, balanced and invigorated.

There are many other such exercises that a Yoga teacher or Qi Gong or Tai Chi teacher could give you. If you are already seeing an acupuncturist and feel you would like help with your breathing and connecting with your energetic body s/he should be able to advise you.

Once you have turned your gaze to look at your physical being and your energetic being you can look inward with an enquiring vision. That is the beginning of meditation and enlightenment.

EXERCISE THREE: BREATHING BEYOND BREATH

This is an exercise used entirely for meditation. In many ways you have been meditating all through the exercises in Chapter Five and through the exercises above. Now you are going to bring a particular focus to doing it.

- *Step One:* Become aware of the flow of breath in and out of your body. You are not trying to breathe deeply – you are simply watching your breath with curiosity, its coming and going.
- *Step Two:* Become aware of the moment between breaths, the still-point of the body when it balances its needs with the needs of the environment. Enter as deeply as you are able into the stillpoint – seeking out in it the moment when the next inhalation begins and the place that it begins from.
- *Step Three:* Remain in this state of relaxed awareness bringing more and more attention to the still-point. You are actively seeking the beginning of the next breath within this moment of stillness.
- Then there is not another point – there is a gradual flowing towards the question, 'What is breathing me?' That question does not arise without the answer. To find the answer one has to remain with the breath and with the question.

VOICE: THE SOUND OF BREATH

There are many other ways to connect with and use the breath as a means of meditation. Personally I am a great believer in chanting although not many breathworkers introduce it into their work – it is usually seen as a separate branch of work with voice. However, chanting does have the effect of slowing down the exhalation and arresting hyperventilation.

Here is a simple technique you can try:

- Again sitting in a supported and comfortable position do a few whispered 'Ahhhhs' of the Alexander Technique. Breathe in and as you breathe out allow the breath to flow from the mouth with the whispering ahhhh, as if you are making a very long sigh. This will relax the jaw.
- When you feel ready you are going to breathe out through your mouth now making the sound 'Aaaaaaaaa . . .'(as in rather) engaging your voice. Let the sound resonate in your mouth and the back of your throat. Allow the sound to continue as long as you are breathing out. Feel the abdominal muscles engaging to 'hold' the sound of your voice up, to lend it strength. Repeat this about four or five times then go back to the whispered 'ahhhh'.
- Take a few relaxed breaths before engaging the voice again. Now you can move on to make 'ng' sound by blocking the back of your palate with your tongue to make an 'ng' sound (as in chanting). Hold the ng sound as long as possible – just as with the aaaaah – but this time allow the sound to resonate in your sinus cavities and head. Repeat it a few times then go back to the whispered 'ahhhh'.

Using the voice in this way allows the mind to calm down, it slows down the breathing and puts one in an ideal attitude for meditation and conscious breathing.

It is appropriate to end this chapter with a quote from the great breathwork teacher, Ilse Middendorf:

Breath is a connecting force. It creates a bodily equilibrium and balance and helps us to make inner and outer impressions interchangeable. It connects the human being with the outside world and the outside world with the inner world. Breathing is an original unceasing movement and therefore actual life. The ineffable has given nature various autonomous laws which have still to come to fruition. Experiencing the breath means to start to live in a new way. Breathing became the 'guide rope' that enabled me to lead the body and with it the spiritual and mental into a new 'opening' to life where meaning is to achieve a wider consciousness and greater expansion in the inner and outer spaces.[1]

1. Ilse Middendorf. *Bone, Breath and Gesture.*

PRINCIPLES OF BREATHWORK

UNFOLDING EMBODIMENT

> I have been trying to imagine a framework for the origin of life, guided by a personal philosophy which considers the primal characteristics of life to be homeostasis rather than replication, diversity rather than uniformity, the flexibility of the cell rather than the tyranny of the gene, the error tolerance of the whole rather than the precision of the parts . . . the qualitative features which I consider essential: looseness of structure and tolerance of errors.
>
> FREEMAN DYSON

I f we read none of this book or any other book on breathing our bodies would continue to breathe. However, once we have *discovered* how deeply personal breathing is – how much it is linked to what we are feeling, thinking and who we are with and in touch with, just breathing can never be the same again. Then it becomes our bridge: our bridge from the conscious to the unconscious; from life to death; from unknowing to knowing.

We are not a part of this particular environment on earth accidentally: its formation and growth led to us: complex human beings breathing in its atmosphere and breathing out ourselves. It is as the great mythical bird, Bhasund, he who is the Master of Masters of Breathing, says in the Yoga of Vasistha:

As you breathe in the world breathes out, and with your out-breath the world is able to breathe in.

We can transport ourselves from this planet and float in space, even live in space, and maybe one day we will colonize other planets. But we will always have to replicate the exact atmosphere and environment that we have on this planet, for we can live in no other. Embracing this means embracing breath not only as a means to self-knowledge but as a bridge to all knowledge, because breath binds us to each other and to the past and the future. Remember, the atmosphere is not replaced – the one we have now has evolved with us from our beginning and will continue to evolve with the air we have breathed out long after we have died and are being carried through and to all parts of the planet on the winds that sweep it.

We can use our breathing to help direct us in our own personal unfoldment. To do that we will need the help and guidance of those who themselves have walked some way on the road to piercing the mystery of breath. In this chapter we will look at the possibilities.

THE WAY FORWARD – AND BACKWARD

YOGA

Yoga is an excellent place to begin an exploration of breathing. After many years of practising it I am convinced that all the postures of Yoga are there to challenge the way we breathe and forge new breathing habits in our bodies. If you want to explore your breathing because you are suffering from chronic fatigue syndrome or the TATT – Tired All The Time – syndrome, Yoga is an excellent place to start. However, there is no uniformity of teaching in Yoga so I would strongly suggest you begin by contacting your local adult education authority and asking if you can speak to some of the teachers. Ask them about their particular methodology and how much of its focus is on breathwork. Some of the systems of Yoga have become 'exercise and power' oriented and you will have to do some phonework or legwork to find the right teacher for your needs.

TAI CHI AND CHI GONG

There has been an explosion of interest in these two systems in the last decade. While neither directly focuses on breathing they use movement with breath to bring our attention to our breathing. In fact, if I am unable to recommend a Yoga teacher in an area I usually advise that the person seeks out a Tai Chi or Chi Gong teacher because these two systems have stayed closer to their traditional roots than Yoga has since its transport to Western soil. They both provide more of a 'bodywork' environment than an exercise one. Tai Chi is actually a martial art but it employs balance and focused attention rather than physical strength. Chi Gong is a system of movement that developed along with acupuncture to correct the imbalance of Qi in the system. Its movements are gentle, opening and explorative rather than goal-seeking and imposing – all ideal for exploring your breathing.

THE ALEXANDER TECHNIQUE

If you have felt through the exercises in this book that you have a great deal of physical tension that you are unable to dispose of yourself it would be advisable to get help. I have seen the Alexander Technique work absolute wonders for people where tension was so locked into muscle that they were not even aware of its existence. The Alexander Technique is taught by a teacher who will recommend a course of sessions for you to attend. Each session usually lasts about three-quarters of an hour but its effect can be felt for days.

Alexander himself once declared, 'I got them to release in spite of themselves' when talking about some students. That is exactly what it feels like – the muscles give up their tension because the teacher, through guided movement, helps you to stop holding onto it!

HAKOMI

This is a relatively new and extremely exciting body-oriented psychotherapy. Developed by Ron Kurtz in the mid-1970s it was a culmination of his previous study and experience in psychology, science and philosophy. His great influences were Bioenergetics and some of the ancient philosophies from the East, particularly Daoism and Buddhism. To quote Mr Kurtz from his book, *The Hakomi Method:*

> The body mobilizes to deal with situations as the mind understand them. In this way the body reflects mental life.

The beauty of Hakomi is that it allows you to explore, in the safest possible environment, the way your body has organized itself around your life experiences, including breathing.

MEDITATION

There are now many schools of meditation all over England. Some Yoga teachers have a particular interest in meditation and may include it as part of their classes. All techniques of meditation will focus on the breath. Quite well advertised is the Buddhist *Vipassana* meditation. The different schools of Buddhism will each differ in their particular emphasis on Vipassana. One way of translating the Sanskrit word Vipassana is, 'sitting still and seeing many things'. One of the 'things' the practitioner will see is their breathing. Mindful breathing is very much a core focus of this method.

The Reverend Thich Nhat Hanh, who has a centre in France but whose books are available everywhere, was one of the first teachers to make available the Buddhist techniques of mindful breathing. His works would be a good starting point of your journey if you wish to explore your breathing through meditation.

OPENING THE DOOR

A good place to end this introduction to breathing is with a story. The stories that have survived of heroes and demons and ordinary people becoming either, are one of the ways we have preserved great truths in our many and diverse cultures. I heard this story from Father Daniel Berrigan, an American Jesuit priest, who was told it by the Reverend Thich Nhat Hanh, a Vietnamese Buddhist monk. Now, here I am, a Hindu monk, offering it to you with all the humility that this great story, with its golden nugget of truth, deserves. I am honoured to have been one of its keepers. The story goes like this:

1

A man leaves the village of his birth to seek happiness elsewhere. He travels for a long time looking for a place of happiness. After many moons he comes to a village set in a beautiful valley that is washed by gentle streams and rivers. The people of the village are smiling and welcoming – his heart sings for he has found his place. He settles down in the village and marries a young lady. They are blissfully happy in their home, and in the common fields that they work each day with the rest of the village. As the years pass only one thing mars their happiness: they are without child. They go each day to the village shrine to make offerings and pray for a child. Their prayers are eventually answered and the wife, though ageing, gives birth to a fine healthy son. They are complete

– all bliss is theirs. As their son begins to grow the only troubling thing is that they hear of war far off. As time passes and distressed travellers trudge wearily through their village they realize the war is growing closer. Just then a messenger comes from the man's home village to tell him that his father has died and that as the eldest son he must come home to perform the customary funeral rights. He is reluctant to leave his beloved wife and son, especially with war clouds gathering. But the villagers assure him they will look out for his family and the disgrace of not going would be too great. The man hurries off back to his birth village. He performs the rites as quickly as custom will allow and then sets off back home. As he comes over the crest of the mountain his heart stops. There, where his beloved village was, is a column of dark black smoke. Screaming he runs down the mountain towards his home. It is gone – nothing but charred stone and wood remain. No-one is there, everyone has been killed or fled. He is mad with despair and walks around the area where his home was, picking up bits of brick and shattered clay pots. Then, among the remains he discovers bones – bones that look as if they could have belonged to a boy the age of his son. Knowing that this is all he has left he picks among the ashes and gathers all the young bones he can find, puts them in a bag and hangs it around his neck – this is all he has left of his beloved son. Then he leaves the village – the place of his greatest joy and now his greatest sorrow. The war sweeps through the land and along with many others he wanders from place to place for many many years – carrying nothing, caring for nothing except the bag of bones of his beloved son around his neck. He eventually grows sick and tired and a villager takes pity on him and offers him shelter in his small barn. The man stays for a few nights, sitting by the fire hugging his bag of bones. One night an urgent knocking comes on the door. The man jumps, startled, frightened. The war has made thieves out of good men. 'Who is it?' He calls out. A voice

answers, 'It is your son.' The man stops. 'My son is dead,' he
replies, hugging his bag of bones. 'No, I escaped and I have been
following you all the years trying to catch up with you, let me
in.' The man hesitates, he feels the weight of the bones – but . . .
Could it be? No!

'My son is dead.'

'No father I am alive – open the door – let me in.'

Can it be? The man strokes the bag around his neck. Could it
be? No, surely not, it is a thief trying to get in.

'Go away my son is dead.'

The knocking and the voice persist for some time and then
become silent.

That is where the story ends. Each of us has at the door of our
consciousness, the breath knocking – urging us to discover the
truth: the truth about our own wholeness, our connectedness,
our reality. Each of us has the choice to open the door and
investigate, to see for certain what the truth is – or to keep
clinging to the past in uncertainty.

This benign universe has offered the breath as the gentlest of
knocks for us to respond to. Whether we open the door or not –
we are responding. It is in our hands – and in our breath.

RESOURCES

FINDING A YOGA TEACHER

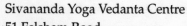

UK

The Yoga for Health Foundation
Ickwell Bury
Biggleswade
Bedfordshire
SG18 9EF
Tel: 01767 627271

Sivananda Yoga Vedanta Centre
51 Felsham Road
Putney
London
SW15 1AZ
Tel: 0181 780 0160

The British Wheel of Yoga
1 Hamilton Place
Boston Road
Sleaford
Lincolnshire
NG34 7ES
Tel: 01529 303233

The Iyengar Yoga Institute
223a Randolph Avenue
London
W9 1NL
Tel: 0171 624 3080

The Yoga Biomedical Trust
156 Cockerell Road
Cambridge
CB4 3RZ
Tel: 01223 367301

USA

The Yoga Journal Magazine
2054 University Avenue
Berkeley, CA 94704
Tel: 510 841 9200

Yoga International's Guide to Yoga Teachers and Classes
RR1, Box 407
Honesdale, PA 18431
Tel: 800 821-YOGA

USA

Gay Hendricks
The Hendricks Institute
409 East Bijou Street
Colorado Springs
CO 80903
Tel: 800 688 0772

Somatic Resources
PO Box 2067
Berkeley
CA 94702
Tel: 510 540 7600

The Middendorf Breath Institute
198 Mississippi
San Francisco
CA 94107
Tel: 415 255 2174

BODY CENTRED PSYCHOTHERAPY

UK

Hakomi UK
18 South Street
Lewes
East Sussex
Tel: 01273 706511

The Hakomi Institute
PO Box 1873
Boulder
CO 80306
Tel: 303 499 6699

The Rosenberg-Rand Institute of Integrated Body
  Psychotherapy
Venice
CA

THE ALEXANDER TECHNIQUE

UK

Society of Teachers of the Alexander Technique
10 London House
266 Fulham Road
London
SW10 9E1
Tel: 0171 351 0828

THE BUTEYKO METHOD

The Hale Clinic
7 Park Crescent
London
W1N 3HE
Tel: 0171 631 0156

HYPERBARIC OXYGEN

UK

The Hyperbaric Oxygen Trust
Ryton House
Primrose Lane
Forest Row
East Sussex
RH18 5LT
Tel: 01342 825467

USA

Ocean Hyperbaric Centre
4001 Ocean Drive
Lauderdale-by-the-Sea
FL 33308
Tel: 954 771 4000

Texas A & M University Hyperbaric Oxygen Laboratory
A.P. Beutal Health Centre
College Station
TX 77843-1264
Tel: 409 845 5031

MEDITATION

London Buddhist Centre
51 Roman Road
London
E2 0HU
Tel: 0181 981 1225

The Reverend Thich Nhat Hanh
Village des Pruniers
Meyrace
47120 Loubes-Bernac
France
Tel: 33 (0)16 53 96 75 40

FURTHER READING

YOGA AND BREATHWORK

Kent, Howard. *Breathe Better, Feel Better,* (Apple)
Johari, Harish. *Breath, Mind and Consciousness,* (Destiny Books)

PERSONAL DEVELOPMENT AND BREATHWORK

Gray, John. *Your Guide to the Alexander Technique,*
  (Victor Gollancz Ltd)
Timmons and Ley, eds. *Behavioral and Psychological Approaches
  to Breathing Disorders,* (Plenum Press)
Hendricks, Gay. *Conscious Breathing: Breathwork for Health,
  Stress Release and Personal Mastery,* (Bantam Books)
Brown, Malcolm. *The Healing Touch,* (LifeRhythm)
Hanlon Johnson, Don, ed. *Bone, Breath and Gesture: Practices of
  Embodiment,* (North Atlantic Books)
Kurtz, Ron. *Hakomi: Body-centred Psychotherapy,* (LifeRhythm)
Boerstler and Kornfeld, *Life To Death: Harmonizing the
  Transition,* (Healing Arts Press)

THE BODY–MIND CONNECTION

Sheldrake, Rupert. *A New Science of Life*
  (Paladin Grafton Books)
Chopra, Deepak. *Quantum Healing,* (Bantam Books)
Ornstein, Robert and Sobel, David. *The Healing Brain,*
  (Papermac)

Brockman, John and Matson, Katinka, eds. *How Things Are: A Science Toolkit for the Mind*, (Weidenfeld and Nicolson)
Churchland, Paul M. *Matter and Consciousness*, (The MIT Press)
Pert, Candace B. *Molecules of Emotion*, (Scribner)

ASTHMA AND BREATHING

Stalmatski, Alexander. *Freedom From Asthma: Buteyko's Revolutionary Treatment*, (Kyle Cathie Limited)

HYPERBARIC OXYGEN THERAPY

Neubauer and Walker. *Hyperbaric Oxygen Therapy: Using HBOT to Increase Circulation, Repair Damaged Tissue, Fight Infection, Save Limbs and Relieve Pain*, (Avery Publishing Group)

BREATHING AWARENESS TAPES

Ambikananda, Swami. *Conscious Breathing: The Bridge to the Unconscious*, (The Traditional Hatha Yoga Foundation, 18 Westminster Way, Earley, Reading)

MEDITATION AND BREATHING

Nhat Hanh, Thich. *The Blooming of a Lotus*, (Beacon Press)
Ambikananda, Swami. *Meditation: Its Breath and Soul*, tape and booklet published by the Traditional Hatha Yoga Foundation